Bollywood Weddings

Bollywood Weddings

Dating, Engagement, and Marriage in Hindu America

Kavita Ramdya

LEXINGTON BOOKS
A division of
ROWMAN & LITTLEFIELD PUBLISHERS, INC.
Lanham • Boulder • New York • Toronto • Plymouth, UK

Published by Lexington Books
A division of Rowman & Littlefield Publishers, Inc.
A wholly owned subsidiary of The Rowman & Littlefield Publishing Group, Inc.
4501 Forbes Boulevard, Suite 200, Lanham, Maryland 20706
www.lexingtonbooks.com

Estover Road, Plymouth PL6 7PY, United Kingdom

British Library Cataloguing in Publication Information Available

Library of Congress Cataloging-in-Publication Data

The hardback edition of this book was previously cataloged by the Library of Congress as follows:

Ramdya, Kavita.
  Bollywood weddings : dating, engagement, and marriage in Hindu America / Kavita Ramdya.
    p. cm.
  Includes bibliographical references and index.
  1. Hindu marriage customs and rites—United States. 2. Hindus—United States. I. Title.
  BL1226.82.M3R36 2010
  392.5089'91411073—dc22

                                                                                    2009039582
ISBN: 978-0-7391-3854-0 (cloth : alk. paper)
ISBN: 978-0-7391-3855-7 (pbk : alk. paper)

⊖™ The paper used in this publication meets the minimum requirements of American National Standard for Information Sciences—Permanence of Paper for Printed Library Materials, ANSI/NISO Z39.48-1992.

Printed in the United States of America

Contents

Acknowledgments

First, I am grateful to Dr. Stephen Prothero for his enthusiasm and support in my PhD dissertation project, writing about weddings in a way that is academically rigorous without sacrificing the human elements of my participants' stories. Big thanks to Dr. Nazli Kibria whose seemingly endless reading suggestions provided the solid foundation from which to write my own research. Thank you, Boston University's Graduate School of Arts and Sciences, for awarding me the Presidential University Graduate Fellowship which covered my tuition cost, provided me with a stipend, and gave me the opportunity to teach history, literature, and writing on a university level. Additionally, I want to acknowledge the educators that inspired me to pursue my education to the highest level: Mr. Michael Shelley, Dr. Peter V. Rajsingh, and Dr. Anita Patterson. Thank you all for your mentorship and support over the years. Thanks to Dr. Xufei Jin who advised me to write about the Asian-American experience. Without the twenty couples who invited me to their weddings and into their homes, this book would be nothing. The Indian-American community continues to inspire me, a sentiment I hope is captured in my work. Of course, without the unconditional love of my parents and support from my brother I would not be where I am today. Thank you, Mom and Dad, for your enthusiasm in everything I do. And for giving me my dream wedding. Last but not least, thank you to my husband, Mansoor, the only man suitable for me to marry. This book is dedicated to my mother, with whom I talked about marriage from when I was a young girl.

Introduction

On a fortuitously warm evening in September 2005 that overturned all my family's and friends' expectations that I would have a conventional Indian-Hindu wedding, I married my husband in an outdoor civil ceremony at a country club in Long Island, New York. Marrying in an outdoor civil ceremony was not a decision that came easily to me. In fact the dissimilar cultural and religious backgrounds of my husband and me made it impossible for me to picture our wedding day for much of the time we were seriously dating.

Mansoor was born and raised in Trinidad where he grew up in a devoutly Muslim home; his grandmother taught him how to read the Quran in Arabic, and he ate only halal meat (meat prepared in a manner prescribed by Islamic law). Whereas I grew up dancing garba (a Gujarati group dance) at Indian wedding receptions (while my dad sipped Jack Daniel's on the rocks with his friends), alcohol and dancing were absent from the weddings my husband attended. In Muslim weddings, the bride wears white, and guests are strictly segregated by gender. At Hindu weddings, the bride wears a bright red sari (traditional formal Indian attire for women) and family and friends of both genders mingle and chatter. How could I possibly plan a wedding that would satisfy the expectations of both sets of parents and their extended families, not to mention the desire of my husband and myself to express our feelings for each other on our wedding day?

To make a long story short, we had a Muslim wedding ceremony in which Mansoor's uncle performed the role of the imam, followed by a halal, buffet Indian dinner. Mansoor wore a kufi skull cap, and I covered my hair with the dupatta (scarf) that accompanied the white lengha (fitted skirt and top Indian outfit) I wore. Nine months later, in a custom-made gown made of two golden saris (I designed it myself), my parents walked me down the aisle (Figure 1). We recited vows we wrote together and concluded the ceremony with a kiss. The reception was a sit-down dinner (Broiled Filet of Salmon with Dill Hollandaise Sauce, Roasted Free Range Chicken basted with Lemon and Rosemary, Chateaubriand with a Five Peppercorn Sauce and a Grilled Vegetable Tower were menu options) and for a party favor was an almond-flavored mithai (Indian sweets). The emcee sang Frank Sinatra classics, and the deejay closed the reception with "Mundian To Bach Ke" a Punjabi Bhangra song mixed to the beat of the *Knight Rider* theme.

Mystified by the lack of adherence to traditional Hindu wedding custom, friends and family later interrogated me as to why I did not marry in a Hindu wedding ceremony. Up until that point I had always assumed that my peers, second-generation Indian-American Hindus, secretly wished for a wedding like mine: one where they could express both their American identity as well as their Indian background. However, through conversations with family and friends, I realized that my wish for a hybrid Indian-American wedding day was the anomaly. My peers almost exclusively desired a wedding that would adhere to age-old Hindu tradition followed by a western-style reception.

Thus began my quest for understanding why and how second-generation Indian-American Hindus living and working in arguably the most diverse and media-driven place in the United States, New York City, could possibly escape the seductive nature of mainstream American wedding culture, a tradition that emphasizes romantic love and the couple's union over ancient customs which adhere to strict religious codes that felt so distant from the way my peers and I lead our lives.

Second-generation Indian-American Hindus, while making up a small fraction of the U.S. population, are an exceptional group. Although the Asian Indian minority makes up less than one percent of the total U.S. population according to the most recent *American Community Survey* report about Asian Americans, it is still the second most populous Asian ethnic group in the United States (behind the Chinese). The second generation accounts for twenty-seven percent of the Asian Indian population in America, and the community is making its presence known on professional, cultural, political, artistic, and social landscapes.[1] The 2004 *American Community Survey* administered by the Department of Commerce reports two-thirds of Asian Indians hold college and graduate degrees and three-fifths work as professionals and in management positions. Asian Indian families earn the highest median household income of all Asian households, taking home ten thousand dollars more than the median income and making on average seventy thousand dollars per household. Although Indians are still a small minority and an anomalous one for their financial and educational success, examining Indians in America illuminates features of the steadily growing population. It also reveals much about what it is to be American.

Weddings are a useful cultural phenomenon for understanding American values and how ethnic Americans adopt, adapt, and occasionally reject them. In a prototypical mainstream middle-class American wedding, the bride personalizes her wedding festivities with her favorite flowers, a self-designed wedding program, and choice of music.[2] Common components of the mainstream American wedding include a flower girl gingerly tossing petals along the aisle, a trail of best men and bridesmaids walking in a procession, the father-of-the-bride giving his daughter away to her future husband, the exchanging of rings and possibly vows between the bride and groom, and a kiss to seal the couple's marital union. Guests are focused on the couple; both the bride and the groom say and show that they are willing and active participants of their marriage and express their love for one another in their vows sealed with a kiss. Witnesses from the community are there simply to observe what the couple is doing. Universal components of the mainstream American wedding reception include the deejay's enthusiastic introduction of the newlyweds, the newlywed's first dance, the parents' dance, the bouquet toss, and the cake cutting. This type of wedding will seem "natural" to many American readers, but it is of course a product of culture and history that expresses such American values such as independence and agency.

Traditional Hindu weddings express a very different philosophy toward the couple in relation to the community. *Vivaha*, or marriage, is one of the most significant *samskaras* (rites of passage) in Hinduism. In a traditional Hindu wedding, the couple does not openly and willingly express their love in front of their community; in fact, the couple never speaks at all. The bride and bridegroom have next to no role in their wedding save following the instruction of the priest, parents and extended family while guests often seem not to be paying attention, frequently talking amongst themselves, feasting on samosas (potato-filled fried appetizers) and drinking chai (Indian tea). Shared components of a typical Indian-Hindu wedding are the following: a *baraat* where the groom arrives at the wedding site on a horse accompanied by friends and family, the *suswgatam* where the bride's mother welcomes and the bride garlands the groom, Ganesh *puja* (prayer) where the priest invokes Lord Ganesh, *kanya pravesh* where the bride is escorted to the mandap by a maternal uncle, *kanyadan* where the bride's father places his daughter's right hand in the groom's right hand, *mangalsutra bandhan* where the bride and groom tie a religious thread around one another, and *sapta-padi* where the couple takes seven steps together around the sacred fire. While some of the components of a typical Hindu ceremony have analogies in the mainstream white American one, many of the traditions above have no distinct parallel to the familiar Judeo-Christian wedding.

I recognize that there is diversity within the general Hindu community. Punjabis differ from Gujaratis. Shiva worship differs from Krishna worship. The diversity among Hindus is a variable in my book: there are no generic Hindus. However, in the United States there is a more generic brand of Hinduism. In the 1960s, during the Brain Drain, Indians from different regions stuck together. American Hindu temples became places where all Indian Hindus could worship together.

Common components in an Indian wedding reception are dance performances by the couple's friends and family, feasting on a buffet-style Indian dinner, and group dances to the tunes of bhangra, percussion music that originates from Punjab, and Bollywood music. The couple does not design their own wedding and personalize it the way American couples frequently do. Yet it is not the case that second-generation Indian-American Hindus are not influenced, or perhaps seduced, by American wedding traditions, particularly since Americans of Hindu Indian origin have been so successful in integrating themselves in other avenues of mainstream American life.

Sixty percent of Asian Indian adults in the United States are married.[3] The specific phenomenon I am interested in examining is *how* middle to upper class Indian-American Hindu men and women negotiate the Hindu wedding ritual, including the marriage decision process.[4] This book begins with the second generation's process of finding a spouse. It moves through the engagement process, and concludes on the wedding day.

Although the focus here is negotiating engagement and marriage, I am interested more broadly in the negotiation of culture. In *Bollywood Weddings: Dating, Engagement and Marriage in Hindu America*, I look at marriage to make sense of how second-generation Indian-American Hindus negotiate two vastly different cultures that represent dichotomous sets of values. Indian-Americans play a significant role in the workings of the national economy, and I believe that understanding their values in terms of conflicts and compromises between traditional Indian-Hindu and American ones will prove important in our understanding of them. Understanding this population, in turn, will help us understand American culture since it is often by bumping up against competing values that, individually and communally, we learn what our values are.

Whereas originally I situated second-generation Indian-American Hindus between two antithetical philosophies, that of prototypical mainstream middle-class America and traditional India, my research repeatedly frustrated this worthy assumption, prompting me to extend and complicate my thesis to include modern-day Bollywood as a prominent mediating source of culture informing second-generation Indian-American Hindus on their wedding day. Not two but three cultures are operating in the lives of second-generation Indian-American Hindus when they are planning their weddings: a traditional India which in some respects no longer exists in the most pluralistic country in the world but which has a presence in the immigrant and second generation's memories and sense of history, mainstream middle-to-upper class America as described in wedding planning magazines such as *Modern Bride* and websites such as *theknot.com*, and Bollywood India as instantiated by wedding-planning magazines such as *Bibi* and websites such as *benzerworld.com*. All of these cultures are inventions of a sort, existing, perhaps, as much in magazines and on the silver screen as in real life. But all are real insofar as they tug on the subjects of my study who negotiate between three cultures.

Ironically, the Bollywood movie industry, where the immigrant and second generation can conceive of romance and love marriage in India, is the terrain upon which both generations collect inspiration when planning an Indian wedding in America. Bollywood culture is of course Indian, since the films that constitute it are produced largely in Mumbai, consumed by Indians, and articulate what viewers believe to be "Indian" values and norms. But Bollywood is also a recent phenomenon influenced (as the name indicates) by Hollywood and by American ways of seeing the world and living in it. Bollywood, the unexpected third culture to emerge in my research, is the mediating culture between pre-modern India and present-day America, tradition and modernity, East and West.

Another surprising conclusion I came to is that a pre-arranged wedding culture already exists for second-generation Indian-American Hindus. An established structure for organizing the wedding day presented itself in all the weddings I attended. Additionally, the family's involvement in planning the festivities, the aesthetic options for decorating the wedding, and even the ways in which a "boy" or "girl" could find a suitable match are long established in the community. My peers do not need to invent a wedding culture. And very little innovation after forty years of establishing an Indian community in the United States is required.

I studied twenty couples, sixteen of which included husbands and wives who were both Hindus and four of which were bi-cultural. (Khyati Joshi's interviews of forty-one second-generation Indians led her to conclude that most Indian Americans "emphasized the importance of finding a coethnic, coreligionist spouse" which is reflected in the challenges I experienced in finding bi-cultural couples.[5] Among all four of the bi-cultural couples I met, the Indian-American Hindu women were married to white American men). I asked participants about their experiences of marrying as Hindus in America in order to shed light on how second-generation Indian-American Hindus make sense of Hinduism, India, America, the world, and themselves. All of the participants had at least college degrees, and seventy-five percent held post-graduate degrees in such areas as finance, law, medicine, academia, journalism, computer science, and dentistry. Few came from single-parent families, and all had experiences traveling to and spending time in India. Every American-born Indian Hindu had strong ties with nuclear and extended family members. All were professionals successful in their chosen field.

My research led me to draw many conclusions about the second generation's worldview, including its association of tradition, sobriety and seriousness with India and romance, love, and celebration with America despite their integration of Bollywood culture into their cultural lives and wedding day. Whereas initially I hoped to explore dichotomies of values such as communitarianism versus individualism, extended family versus nuclear family, elder-oriented culture versus youth-oriented culture, and tradition versus innovation, I found that dichotomous relationships such as the ones listed above no longer apply for a second generation that draws on age-old Indian traditions, mainstream modern American customs, and the hybrid of the two known as Bollywood.

Defining Terms

Abandoning the dichotomies listed above that did nothing to illuminate the ideas that emerged from my research, I coined phrases that describe what motivates the second-generation Indian-American Hindus in planning their weddings. The first phrase is "occasional Hindus" which describes almost all of my participants. My subjects are middle-to-upper class, well-educated professionals who live or work in New York. They lead lives quite similar to their non-Asian American, urban-dwelling peers. Whereas for the immigrant-generation Indian Hindus whose religious lives are part of their daily life, for my participants, religious life is largely a memory; after a childhood of attending temple and celebrating Hindu holidays, all of which were organized by their parents, the second generation seems to participate in Hindu rituals only on occasion, usually during rites of passage such as engagement and marriage. Few set up a domestic religious shrine that resembles the ones popular in first-generation homes, and, even as adults, none of the second generation was motivated to pray or participate in a Hindu ritual without their parents' motivation and accompaniment. The second generation, rather than integrating prayer and religious devotion into their daily lives, instead expresses Hinduness at symbolic moments. In short, this is life cycle religion, a form of

Hinduism not unlike the Catholicism of those who attend a church at Baptism, marriage and death.

Another finding of my study is that displaying Hinduness does not function as a rejection of an American identity. Religion scholar Prema Kurien in "Becoming American by Becoming Hindu" (1998) asserts that having a distinctly religious Hindu upbringing is a key socializing process by which second-generation Indian-American Hindus develop their identity as hyphenated Americans rather than rejecting Americanness. Kurien describes Hindu Americans as having an identity inclusive rather than exclusive of their religious beliefs. Like Hinduism, according to Kurien, ethnicity is socially acceptable in the United States. Displaying Hinduness underscores rather than undermines Americanness. In post-civil rights America, old stereotypes that Americans have to give up culture and religion no longer hold true. America's romance with culture is true in particular with relation to model minorities.

However, whereas Kurien posits that religiosity is alive and well among Hindu immigrants and their children, my findings show otherwise: whereas maintaining a Hindu religious identity is a priority among first-generation Indian-American Hindus, the second generation is only "occasionally Hindu." I speculate there are a number of reasons why the second-generation Indian-American Hindus I met were only "occasional Hindus." First, the men and women I met are young, all between twenty-four and thirty-nine years old. Perhaps when they age and begin having children of their own they will return to more active religiosity. Second, the men and women I met are middle-to-upper class; they are wealthy, often making a combined six-digit annual salary. It may be that the level of ease with which they have succeeded education-wise and financially in America has kept religiosity from taking a prominent place in their daily lives. Additionally, second-generation Indian-American Hindus may hesitate from participating in rituals because they fear their lack of fluency in Hindi or another Indian dialect will impede them from performing the rituals correctly. Finally, second-generation Indian-American Hindus expressed self doubt in having the knowledge to engage in Hindu rituals "correctly" without their parents or elder's guidance.

In addition to describing second-generation Indian-American Hindus I met as "occasional Hindus," I also observed them displaying "symbolic ethnic capital" during their search for a spouse, at the engagement, and during the wedding day. "Symbolic ethic capital" is a notion that draws from H.J. Gans's article "Symbolic Ethnicity: Future of Ethnic Groups and Cultures in America" (1979) which describes how third-generation Americans of European ancestry participate in ceremonies that celebrate rites of passage and who use "consumer goods, [and] notable foods [that act] as ethnic symbols."[6] The appropriation of ethnic symbols situates ethnicity so that it becomes a leisure time activity expressed at key moments. Second-generation Indian-American Hindus accrue symbolic ethnic capital in order to increase their value on the marriage market among other Indians and their parents, and thus more easily acquire a strong marital prospect who likewise expresses symbolic ethnic capital.

Two types of symbolic ethnic capital emerge in my research: Indian and American. An attractive mate is someone who has both types of capital; contrary to some notions of hyphenated ethnicity, the two are not a zero sum. Second-generation Indian-American Hindus walk a fine tightrope while on the marriage market and planning stages of their wedding, constantly vacillating between increasing one account versus the other, balancing one's store of capital versus the other.

Symbolic ethnic capital is descriptive of something important that goes on more broadly in culture. The second generation has crafted a hybrid identity whereby having symbolic ethnic Indian or American capital adheres in a person by virtue of the *things that they do*. Symbolic ethnic capital is a quality of a person or perceptions of persons when they act, speak, or dress in an Indian or American manner. Symbolic ethic capital is something my participants traded in. Cooking chicken korma, playing the tabla, and participating in a Southeast Asian cultural show are examples of ways in which second-generation Indian-American Hindus accrue symbolic ethnic Indian capital. Living independently in New York City, enjoying the city's nightlife, and dating before marriage are ways in which they accrued symbolic ethnic American capital. The first and second generations desire in a prospective mate both symbolic ethnic capital of an Indian sort and symbolic ethnic capital of an American sort. A perfect wife is one who can wear a sari with ease and also makes a six-digit salary working for a management consultating company. A suitable prospective husband is one who leases commercial real estate in the city while speaking in Hindi on the phone to his grandparents in India. In other words, I found that second-generation Indian-American Hindus are largely looking for a spouse that has all the necessary elements that make them an eligible bachelor or bachelorette according to mainstream American standards but who can also act, speak, or dress in an Indian manner.

Marrying an individual with symbolic ethnic Indian and American capital reinforces a second-generation American's own ethnic-American identity. Just as Prema Kurien posits that displaying Hinduness does not function as a rejection of an American identity, I found that a majority of the second-generation Americans I met sought an Indian partner as a way not to reject their Americanness but to express their Americanness. By embracing one's ethnic heritage, the second generation conveyed their American identity as an ethnic one rather than a mainstream one, differentiating them from the American mainstream. Proud of their American identity and exotic cultural and religious backgrounds as well as the minority's success in mainstream America, second-generation Indian-American Hindus were eager to display both their Indianness and Americanness as a way to pronounce their double layered American identity in contrast to their mainstream American peers.

Often, I saw the second generation construct a dichotomous relationship between what they deemed as expressing symbolic ethnic Indian capital and what they deemed as expressing symbolic ethnic American capital. The values they associated with displaying their Indianness consisted of tradition, sobriety, and seriousness, whereas their American values were joy, laughter, and play. This dichotomous relationship between what they considered traditional Indian and American values is demonstrated more plainly when the second-generation Indian-American Hindus had religious, serious and sober wedding ceremonies followed by contemporary, fun wedding receptions.

Key Findings

Showing how second-generation Indian-American Hindus express both American and Indian-Hindu values even as they negotiate their conflicts are my contributions to contemporary studies on South Asian Americans and Hinduism in America. I examine how second-generation Indian-American Hindus adopt, adapt, and reject various elements of the Hindu and mainstream American wedding rituals, including the dating and engagement processes. The first three chapters of this book describe what must happen before the wedding day; key topics include dating, arranged marriage versus love marriage, engagement, and shopping for a Hindu bridal gown.

Chapter 1, "The Marriage Market," asks, "How do second-generation Hindu-Americans negotiate the marriage market?" In it, I describe a hybrid third model called "arranged meetings." This model combines elements of traditional Indian arranged marriage, where parents have unilateral power over whom their child marries, with American love marriage, where two individuals function as free agents in choosing and marrying one another. "Arranged meetings" is not something individual suitors make up on the fly. It is a compromise already negotiated between the first and second generations whereby the second generation filters out prospective marital candidates who will not meet with the first generation's approval, usually through Internet dating websites such as *Shaadi.com* (shaadi is the Hindi word for "marriage").

But once they find candidates who have the "right" religious and ethnic criteria, second-generation Indian-American Hindus pursue American-style courtships where they engage in months and even years of dating, including premarital sex (which is not a part of traditional arranged marriages). Thus, rather than having to choose between a traditional Indian arranged marriage and an American love marriage, the Indian-American Hindus I met integrated the two. The family revolving around second-generation Indian-American Hindus no longer plays a significant role in arranging the meeting between two candidates of marriageable age. This fact speaks to the declining significance of parents and extended family in Indian-American culture and the conformity to Americans' resistance to the norm of deference. Of course, anxieties emerge over this transformation; these anxieties and their resolutions are explored in Chapter 2.

Chapter 2 focuses on how second-generation Indian-American Hindus get engaged. More specifically, it explores whether the second generation has a more typical mainstream American engagement that involves a romantic proposal accompanied by a diamond ring or a traditional Indian one where family members are present and the couple performs *puja* (worship). I found these engagements to operate on two levels: one that is performed for and by the immigrant generation, which is involved in planning the wedding ritual, and one that is more about the bride and bridegroom, which involves the diamond ring and reception.

As in Chapter 1 where I discussed the third model, "arranged meetings," as a mode by which second-generation Indian-American Hindus meet marital prospects, these couples are proceeding in a both/and rather than either/or fashion. They embrace both the private secular American engagement ritual and the public religious Hindu one. Half of the women I met were proposed to with a ring that either followed or preceded a religious ceremony with their family. The engagement proposal is a key moment because it allows Indian-American Hindus to assert both their American identity through the diamond ring proposal and their cultural and religious background through a Hindu ceremony. The secular second-generation Americans I met displayed their Indian-Hindu heritage only on special occasions such as key moments during the engagement and the wedding day, but acting as "occasional Hindus" does not suggest a rejection of Americanness. On the contrary, acting as "occasional Hindus" reinforces their ethnic American identity.

The religious and ethnic flavor of the engagement ceremony usually foreshadowed the nature of the wedding day festivities. Having a religious engagement ceremony also functioned as a much-needed outlet for an immigrant generation anxious about their relative passivity in marrying off a son or daughter. According to tradition, once the children are married, Hindu parents in India can then move onto the next phase in life, which is a full commitment to worship. This retirement stage, or *vanaprastha,* is meant to allow newly-married couples to actively raise their family while the previous generation recedes to the background.

Therefore, in many ways a Hindu marriage is a rite of passage for both the couple and their parents. It commences the couple's contributions to society and serves as the symbolic end of their parents' involvement in their community. American tradition does not include this philosophy; parents are not expected to retreat from their communities and devote themselves to worship. Planning a public engagement party is the immigrant generation's way of endorsing their son or daughter's engagement to friends and family and appearing instrumental in fulfilling their religious obligation to ensure their child marries. Finally, hosting an engagement party for their son or daughter announces the first generation Indian Hindu parents' impending retirement from secular life.

In Chapter 3, I pose the question, "How is India imaginatively constructed in the United States?" Answering this question requires examining America's Indian-Hindu bridal industry. How are symbols of India created and marketed here? What are the pressures from consumer culture to have an "Indian" wedding? I discovered a bridal industry that specifically targets second-generation Indian-American Hindus: in websites such as *WeddingSutra.com* and *benzerworld.com*; in magazines such as *Bibi* and *Shaadi*; and through events such as the Dulhan Expo, where Indian wedding vendors congregate and market bridal fashion, decorations and wedding services to South Asian women.

By focusing on four disparate bridal costumes worn by second-generation Indian-American women, I draw conclusions about what each gown revealed about the bride's identity. In the Hindu tradition, the bride wears a sari chosen by her boyfriend's family; in America the purchase of the dress is a very personal project that the prospective bride engages in herself, perhaps with the *help* of her mother, future mother-in-law and/or bridesmaids. Here too, participants forged a both/and middle path. Second-generation brides neither simply adopted nor simply rejected the American method of finding a wedding outfit. Neither did they adopt or reject the Indian method. Here again an agreement has already been struck between the first and second generations whereby second-generation Indian-American Hindu brides relinquish control over choosing their wedding sari but personally choose their reception outfit. Hamsa's traditional red-and-white ceremony sari and her red-and-gold reception sari; Sachi's white Carolina Herrera couture wedding gown; Ajala's gold lengha; and Savita's red, off-the-rack dress from Macy's allowed me to make conclusions about what wearing ethnic or American garb on a bride's wedding day mean in terms of expressing identity.

The brides I met were eager to purchase ethnic objects to display on their wedding day. In fact, they struggled to purchase their wedding day decorations in India when the identical invitations, party favors and saris were within a half-hour train ride in Jackson Heights, a predominantly-Indian neighborhood in Queens. The influence of Bollywood on contemporary Indian-American Hindu wedding culture also emerges as significant in this portion of the book. Many brides chose to wear lenghas, modern-day skirt and fitted-top ensembles, as opposed to the traditional sari, to their wedding receptions. Rather than research what Courteney Cox or Jennifer Aniston wore on their wedding day as an inspiration for their own wedding gown, second-generation Americans surfed Indian-American wedding websites which showcase bridal worn by Bollywood starlets.

A final conclusion is that orchestrating a properly ethnic-American Hindu wedding is impossible without financial means. A visit to India alone starts at two-thousand dollars round trip, and that is before the wedding shopping begins. Between the religious invitations, the wedding sari, ethnic party favors, the Indian deejay, the wedding mandap, and all the other props necessary in a Hindu wedding ceremony, the expense associated with having an Indian Hindu wedding is beyond those without means. Ethnic Hindu weddings serve to not only display the couple's ties to India (symbolic ethnic Indian capital), but also their families' affluence and success in America (symbolic ethnic American capital).

The final two chapters in *Bollywood Weddings* describe the pre-wedding and wedding-day rituals of second-generation Indian-American Hindus. Chapter 4, "Pre-Wedding Rituals," focuses on festivities such as the engagement and bachelor parties, mendhi (women's hand painting) party, and sangeet (a pre-wedding ceremony party). Again, while the immigrant generation expects the second generation to participate in traditional, pre-wedding Hindu customs, both generations also embrace mainstream American pre-wedding traditions such as the bridal shower. Both sets of tradition were embraced for the purposes of community-building, a value heavily espoused in Indian households, and allowing members of the second generation to express their Americanness via participating in American traditions as well as traditional Hindu ones. American customs such as the bridal shower as well as Indian ones like the mendhi party simultaneously enable members of the immigrant generation to display their success at adapting to American society and at indoctrinating their American children to Hindu wedding culture.

In Chapter 5, "The Wedding Day," I focus on the wedding-day festivities, in-

cluding pre-wedding ceremonies like the baraat (the groom's entrance to the wedding ceremony), religious or civil wedding ceremonies, and the wedding reception. Whereas I had initially theorized that the second generation displays Indianness during the wedding ceremony and Americanness during the wedding reception, this theory is too simple. That is because I now conclude that three sources of
culture (modern-day Bollywood, traditional India, and mainstream America) are
at work here during every moment of the wedding day. Whereas a majority of the
couples I met claimed to have planned a traditional Hindu ceremony followed by
an American-style wedding reception, I witnessed a wedding culture that involved
the interaction of these three sets of tradition in varying degrees at any given point
in the wedding day.

In Chapter 5, the first question I answer is, "Which elements of the Hindu
wedding ceremony survive intact or are adapted in weddings among Hindu Americans?" Traditional Hindu weddings have many elements: the baraat, marrying
under a mandap (Figure 2), *sapta-padi* (a seven step rite where the bride follows
her bridegroom around the fire), the garland exchange, and bidhai, a custom where
the bride weeps and says farewell to her family. I found that three conditions con-
tribute to the likelihood that an element of the Hindu wedding ceremony ritual will
be adapted to the American scene: first, the tradition conveys values that resonate
with the second generation; second, the custom has an analog in the mainstream
American wedding and; third, the tradition puts India on display. Customs such
as the baraat and the varmala are popular elements of the Hindu wedding ceremony among the second generation whereas the kunyandan and bidhai have all
but completely vanished in these ceremonies for reasons I explain in Chapter 5.

The second question I answer is, "Which elements of the mainstream American wedding ceremony and reception are second-generation Indian-American
Hindus adapting for their own use?" Whereas in the Hindu ceremony, the couple traditionally does not speak, are second-generation Indian-American Hindu
couples reciting vows? Are brides choosing to smile during their wedding or are
they remaining modest and demure as is the case in traditional Hindu weddings?
Although the couples I met were adamant about staging traditional Hindu wedding ceremonies followed by American-style receptions, I found that elements of
the American wedding ceremony did enter into many of the Hindu ceremonies I
witnessed, including the bride's walk down the aisle, the wedding program, and
the widely-contested kiss between the bride and groom.

I also discuss how second-generation Indian-American Hindus view India
and America as well as which values they associate with each culture. In other
words, by examining how the second generation plans a traditional Indian ceremony and an American-style wedding reception, what is the second generation's
worldview? I found that second-generation Indian-American Hindus associate
play, joy, and celebration with American culture whereas they view Indian culture
as stoic, serious, and traditional. This is a consequence of the first generation's
immigration to the United States during the 1960s, before India moved fiercely
toward modernity and westernization. This dichotomous view of the world does
not hold water, however, given the strong presence on the second generation's
wedding day of Bollywood culture, which bridges the American/Indian divide by

being both Indian and western, both traditional and modern.

The final section of Chapter 5 describes the conglomerate of cultures that inspire wedding reception culture among second-generation Indian-American Hindus. Including cakes with borders that resembles the pattern on a bride's sari, family and friends that perform choreographed dances to Bollywood film songs, and slide shows of a couple's time secretly dating to the Jewish chair dance (which, oddly enough, found its way into four of the twenty receptions I studied as an "American" custom), the wedding reception displays a wild mix of traditional Indian culture, Bollywood culture, and mainstream American wedding culture espoused in magazines such as *Modern Bride*. Public displays of affection are generally absent even in these hybrid wedding ceremonies but emerge during the wedding reception in the form of the father-daughter dances, kisses between the bride and groom, and toasts celebrating the couple's love.

I found that second-generation Indian-American Hindus were doing less improvisation than I had expected. In fact, a basic template emerged in the weddings I attended and viewed on video. Few weddings had genuinely creative moments, perhaps only four in a total twenty. Instead, the couples I met were following standards and expectations already agreed upon by the first and second generations. Long before I embarked on my study, a compromise has already been reached whereby the second generation participates in what it deems to be a traditional Hindu wedding ceremony (arranged to a significant extent by the first generation) while the reception is a place where the second generation can be in charge and celebrate its American identity. The Indian-American community has evolved enough in the last forty years to have established a pre-arranged, dominant wedding culture that evades major conflict and consists of a both/and model which embraces components of both the American and Indian Hindu wedding ceremony and reception. In other words, the men and women I met were not pioneers when planning their weddings. They were enacting an already negotiated wedding culture. For the most part, little variation existed from wedding to wedding. What we are witnessing in this book is not so much an ongoing negotiation as the playing out of a negotiation already struck.

Planning an Indian wedding with all its ethnic objects (for example, the traditional wedding sari, a horse for the baraat, the fire around which the sapta-padi occurs, and Indian food) does not detract from the first and second generation's success in America. Instead, it reinforces it for family and friends alike. The second generation displays an ethnic-American identity that distances it from mainstream Americans who lack a strong cultural identity. Cultural dilution at a moment when marital success rides on expressing ethnic pride is avoided by staging a wedding with an "Indian cap" as one participant describes it. But, ignorant of the interaction of various cultures at every given moment in these rites, the women and men I met viewed America and India as static rather than dynamic, fixed rather than evolving, dichotomous rather than woven.

Approach and Methodology

My methodology in researching and writing *Bollywood Weddings* included four approaches: personal interviews; material analysis of wedding photography and videography; ethnography, or participant observation in Hindu weddings; and traditional methods of research like reading and interrogating the existing body of literature around South Asian American culture, wedding studies, ethnic studies, religious studies, and sociology.

I attended ten weddings. I also watched videos and viewed the photographs from ten more weddings I was unable to witness. At least one member of each couple in the twenty weddings was a second-generation Indian-American Hindu. Only four couples were bi-ethnic couples and, in all four, the bride was a second-generation American whereas the groom was a white male. All forty of my participants were college educated, and seventy-five percent of them held at least one graduate degree; all worked as professionals in such areas as finance, law, medicine, academia, journalism, computer science, or dentistry.

In my book, I perform what anthropologist Clifford Geertz describes in *Interpretation of Culture* (1973) as "thick description." I provide my reader with descriptive information about my participants' search for a marriage partner, their pre-wedding festivities, and their wedding day, all accompanied by my own analysis and interpretation. It is my hope to convey moral, spiritual, and cultural detail in what I have observed and written in my interactions with these couples. But *Bollywood Weddings* is empirical in nature. The conclusions I draw emerged from reporting and investigating the facts presented to me.

In addition to observing, analyzing and writing about weddings among Indian-American Hindus, I interviewed couples upon returning from their honeymoon. I conducted my interviews in my participants' homes; these interviews lasted between ninety minutes and three hours. Questions included asking how the bride and groom met, what role their parents and extended family members took in matchmaking, and who planned their wedding ceremony and reception. These oral histories contained valuable information regarding how the first and second generations plan a Hindu wedding in the United States. In addition to asking questions about their courtship and wedding planning process, I asked my participants questions about their weddings such as how they would describe their wedding dress, the ceremony, and the reception. Participant observation is meant to compare how these couples viewed their wedding in comparison to what I observed when attending these weddings or watching them on video. I used the "snowball" sampling technique where one interview of a couple lead to references to one to three more couples, usually close friends or family members.

Material and visual sources such as Mira Nair's movie *Monsoon Wedding* (2001), Hindu-American matrimonial websites such as *Shaadi.com*, Indian wedding clothing websites such as *Benzerworld.com*, South Asian bridal magazines such as *Bibi*, mainstream American bridal magazines such as *Modern Bride*, and newspapers such as *India Abroad* were significant in my analysis.

I focused on second-generation Indian-American Hindus living or working in New York City and the tri-state area. The 1990 *Census* indicates that 10 percent of the Asian Indian population in the United States lives in New York City while nearly 25 percent of the Asian Indian population resides in the New York City metropolitan area. I count two reasons for my focus on the New York tri-state area: New York is a city that has allowed first-generation Indians to successfully replicate India in the New World, and the city is noted for accommodating varied cultures. These conditions allow second-generation Indian-American Hindus to make life choices with the richness of a cosmopolitan and worldly environment while at the same confining them in the culture of traditional Indian Hindu values circa 1965 to 1975 during which their parents migrated to the United States.

Focusing on second-generation Indian-American Hindus in the New York metropolitan area was easy considering the city is full of Indian-American Hindus working at investment banks, hospitals, universities and consulting firms. However, attending ten weddings and sifting through ten more wedding videos was no easy task. Why attend so many weddings? Why subject myself to watching hours of wedding video? Weddings are a window into seeing how second-generation Indian-American Hindus construct India and America. Weddings reveal conflicts and choices. Finally, weddings matter, not only for the bride and groom. Weddings are rites of passage where intergenerational and cross-cultural tensions play out and, in the case of Indian-American Hindus, convey a sense of compromise between multiple cultures. All of the second-generation Indian-American Hindus I met and whose pre-wedding and wedding day festivities I witnessed or had described to me exemplify the struggle of demonstrating ties to Indian culture and Hindu tradition with expressing an American identity.

Notes

1. U.S. Department of Commerce, *We the People: Asians in the United States*, December 2004 (Washington D.C.: U.S. Census Bureau, 2004), 1-2, 11.

2. Cele C. Otnes & Elizabeth H. Pleck *Cinderella Dreams: The Allure of the Lavish Wedding* (2003), along with bridal magazines such as *Modern Bride* and *Elegant Bride*, inform my discussion of mainstream American bridal culture among the second-generation Indian-American Hindus white peers. In this ideal type, the typical subjects are urban-dwelling, middle-to-upper class, college-educated professionals. I use the writers' descriptions of wedding planning and wedding-day traditions among middle class and affluent Americans as a starting point for my material analysis of weddings among second-generation Indian-American Hindus. The culture of the American wedding is the norm against which I will examine how second-generation Indian-American Hindus negotiate the Hindu wedding ritual. I say American because the culture I am attending to is the culture of *Modern Bride* magazine and the bridal industry. The ideal type of American wedding is not a multi-ethnic one but a mainstream white one.

3. U.S. Department of Commerce, *The Asian American Community: 2004* (Washington D.C.: U.S. Census Bureau, February 2007), 8.

4. I focus my book on middle-to-upper class second-generation Indian Americans raised in Hindu households because I am specifically interested in how the

children of successful professional post-1965 brain drain Indian immigrants negotiate American notions about the wedding ritual and the marriage decision-making
process with traditional Hindu-Indian philosophies behind both.

5. Khyati Y. Joshi. *New Roots in America's Sacred Ground: Religion, Race,
and Ethnicity in Indian America* (New Brunswick, New Jersey: Rutgers University Press, 2006), 42.

6. H.J. Gans, "Symbolic Ethnicity: Future of Ethnic Groups & Cultures in
America," *Ethnic & Racial Studies* 2, no. 1 (1979): 1-20, 10.

The Marriage Market: Choosing a Suitable Boy

For Rati, a defining moment in her search for an Indian-American Hindu husband was when her white boyfriend accused her of "being racist." Rati had just returned from her first trip to India since she was a child. She stayed in the houses of various relatives, family with whom she "picked up from when we last met without skipping a beat." Often she was meeting extended family for the first time and was impressed by the open-armed welcomes. Upon returning from her trip to her home in New York, Rati's interests in Indian culture re-ignited. She revived her love for vegetarian dishes and began taking yoga. Along with continuing her bharatanatyam (classical Indian dance) classes and watching Bollywood films, she began attending the local temple with some international Indian students she met at the local arty theater's showing of *Lagan*, a popular Bollywood film.

Paul, Rati's boyfriend at the time, quietly grew more and more impatient with Rati's love for anything Indian and finally burst out in frustration when he saw her zealotry showed no signs of subsiding. Boarding a local train a few moments before the departure time, Rati made a motion to sit next to an Indian male passenger before Paul intercepted and took the last empty seat himself. Rati was left to stand, but she caught Paul's look of self-satisfied smugness at having successfully kept Rati from making another Indian acquaintance, a man who might serve as a further threat to their relationship. Later, when Rati confronted Paul about his sneakiness as well as his lack of confidence in their relationship, Paul admitted that after dating her he "could never date another Asian again" for fear that he would not be taken seriously since he was not Asian. When pressed further, Paul accused Rati of preferring Indians to whites and of "being a racist."

Rati's anecdote about dating Paul, a white man, is interesting because it highlights the second generation's enthusiasm for and the significance they place on "being Indian" and relying on activities like practicing yoga to express Indianness. Watching Bollywood movies, eating vegetarian, practicing yoga, learning Indian classical dance and other activities are significant in describing the second generation's understanding of India, their own ethnic-American identity and the characteristics they seek in a marriage partner. After the incident described above, Rati dumped Paul and relinquished the American notion of falling in love and pursuing a "love marriage." Shortly thereafter, she posted an online matrimonial ad in shaadi.com. Therein began her adventures and misadventures that would eventually lead her to meet and marry her Indian-American husband, Shiv.

For second-generation Indian-American Hindus, there are two models for marriage: the arranged marriage and the love marriage. These models are diametrically opposed. The love marriage usually involves a whimsical and incidental meeting followed by months and often years of dating. The arranged marriage excludes dating altogether and in fact rarely allows for more than one meeting before the wedding day. When the "boy" and "girl," words used to describe prospective marriage candidates despite their age, profession, or education, meet for the first time, it is usually in a highly-regulated environment where both sets of parents sit in the same room accompanied by supportive extended family members. A wedding follows shortly thereafter, making it the second time the "couple" is allowed to see each other and after which the husband and wife embark on years of "dating" or getting to know one another without the nagging possibility of rejection.

So, how do second-generation Indian-American Hindus negotiate these two opposed models of marriage? How do they reconcile love marriage with arranged marriage? In this chapter I examine courtships among three second-generation Indian-American Hindu couples. This examination led me to discover a middle path, which I call "arranged meetings." "Arranged meetings" is an already negotiated and well-established third model for marrying among second-generation Indian-American Hindus. The second generation uses this method to filter out prospective marital candidates who do not have the "right" ethnic, religious, linguistic, and regional traits desired by their parents. For example, a family active in the Gujurati Hindu community can seek only fellow Gujurati Hindus to introduce to the eligible son or daughter. Any marital candidate left standing is fair game for something akin to dating. The second generation feels free to determine whether the meaningful candidates have sexual chemistry and compatible personalities, characteristically American criteria contemplated in making a "love marriage" decision.

In this way, neither arranged nor love marriage are excluded and the needs and desires of both generations are respected. The first generation is still involved in finding a suitable partner for their child, whether through introductions by family and friends, or placing an ad on-line or in a newspaper. Additionally, candidates who do not come from the same religious sect, speak the desired dialect, or originate from the same region of India (and thus possibly eat dissimilar food), are cast away before a set of eligible prospects are considered. Then second-generation Americans embark in all the activities associated with pursuing an American "love marriage." They date for months and sometimes even years, determining whether she and her partner share common likes and dislikes. They also determine, and not just by holding hands, whether there is enough sexual attraction to keep their mutual attentions "'til death do we part." Along with their immigrant parents, most of the second-generation Indian-American Hindus I met prefer to marry a partner of Indian heritage and Hindu faith because marriage is seen as a definitive way for the second generation to express its identity as ethnic and religious Americans. They are American, yes. But they are also Indian and Hindu. Additionally, pleasing the first generation's wish to see their children marry a Hindu Indian is itself an expression of ethnicity, of one's Indianness, in this case with respect for the traditional value of deference to one's elders.

This idea provides additional ammunition against the "melting pot" metaphor. Within the second-generation Indian-American Hindu ethnic minority, men and women of marriageable age who have high economic and social standing prefer to marry within their community rather than engage in an exogenous marriage. Rather than participate in a "melting pot" as early ethnic scholars described the trajectory of ethnic Americans, participants chose to marry people from within their community despite the New York area's diverse population.

As I described earlier in my discussion of "arranged meetings," rather than debating values and characteristics second-generation Indian-American Hindus should seek in a partner, the first and second generations have already negotiated a compromise whereby the second generation engages in various methods for meeting a partner that meet all or most of the immigrant generation's religious, ethnic, regional, and linguistic cultural criteria. At the same time, the prospects who make it through this sieve of criteria are then free to engage in dating relationships that look typically American. For instance, Shiv and Rati were attracted to each other's profiles because they shared the same regional and religious Indian identity; however, they dated for two years before marrying. Their mutual love for Indian performance was what bonded them together in terms of sharing common interests.

The Indian-Hindu community has evolved enough in the last forty years that mechanisms are already in place for the second generation to search for potential marriage partners. These mechanisms respect both traditional Indian as well as modern American criteria. "Arranged meetings" provide a group of candidates acceptable for a member of the second generation to fall in love with after having satisfied the first generation's ethnic and religious requirements.

Second-generation Indian-American Hindus seek marriage partners who have what I describe as "symbolic ethnic capital." This finding sheds light on how the second generation envisions and understands Hindu India. The men and women in my study scrutinize characteristics in the opposite sex in order to confirm if that marital prospect is "Indian" enough for marriage. Like Rati obsessed over getting better-acquainted with her Indian heritage through practicing yoga, learning Indian classical dance, and watching Bollywood movies, other participants used similar activities as markers for Indian ethnicity among marriage prospects. Being ethnically Indian and from a Hindu family was often not enough. Especially "expressive" Indian-American Hindus desired a marriage partner who could further confirm their identity as Indian-American Hindus.

A number of factors are important in the Indian-Hindu American community when it comes to finding a mate in a limited and dispersed pool of partners. Processes such as placing matrimonial ads in ethnic newspapers and online allow second-generation Indian-American Hindus to meet fellow Americans as well as Indian Hindus in England, Canada, India, and Singapore. These mechanisms are important because they allow second-generation Indian-American Hindus to meet partners that satisfy the first generation's religious and ethnic criteria as well as the community's desire to find a partner with symbolic ethnic Indian and America capital.

Finding a potential partner through newspaper and on-line matrimonial ads was followed by typically American patterns of dating which included a long courtship designed to ferret out similar hobbies and the quality of sexual chemistry. By meeting a potential spouse through a family network or other family-sanctioned modes of pursuing marriage such as online matrimonials, second-generation Indian-American Hindus accrued symbolic ethnic Indian capital they later spent when in long-term relationships and premarital sex. Mainstream American dating was encouraged by my participants' immigrant parents to ensure that romance and love, two values that express Americanness, were as much a part of their children's decision to marry as religious compatibility and regional identity.

Second-generation Indian-American Hindus select future spouses who exhibit Indianness as a way to integrate into America rather than as a way to opt out. The fact that Indianness confirms Americanness helps to explain the dearth of conversation in scholarship and in my interviews regarding issues such as racism and ethnocentrism. The only times my participants ever mentioned racism was in describing their community's reactions against marrying an African American or Muslim. Discussions of racism towards ethnic Indians never surfaced. For the middle-to-upper class Indians I met, status anxieties were relatively low and their lofty socio-economic status enabled obstacles such as racism to recede from their view.

Rati, whose mother is a white Lutheran woman from Canada and whose father is a Hindu raised in Uttra Pradesh, India, literally chose to "be Indian." The story of how Rati decided to utilize shaadi.com, an on-line Internet matrimonial website popular among South-Asian Hindus, supports my notion that, for second-generation Indian-American Hindus interested in expressing their ethnic-American identity, marrying a fellow Indian-ethnic Hindu is the most effective way. Coming from a bi-cultural family, Rati was not exposed to Indian-Hindu culture until her twenties, when she made conscious efforts to adopt Indian-Hindu religion and customs. Rati is both a career-minded professional dancer and an Indian-American woman seeking to establish a family to uphold the Indian and American sides of her identity.

Although Rati's father's family members in Uttar Pradesh were strict Hindus and her mother's family religious Lutherans (Rati's grandfather is a Lutheran pastor), neither Rati nor her younger brother and sister were raised with religion. Rati explains that her father, being the eldest son, "got a lot of western education: British boarding schools" and as an engineer thought "more scientifically and logically than religiously." Since he was fluent in English, none of Rati and her siblings knew Hindi. Rati reasons that her father resisted teaching his children Hindi out of fear of isolating them from their community since in the mid-70s there were few Indians in the Midwestern city in which they lived. Both he and his wife had a cavalier attitude towards providing a religious education to their children. Rati reports that her parents' attitude was: "When you want [religion] in your life, you'll go find what works for you." But Rati's father's decision not to teach his children Hindi or Hinduism goes against the grain of how most Indian immigrants raise their children.

People who are given lots of freedom and choice as children often "rebel" by becoming conservative, embracing traditions their parents have left behind. Rati and her father's contrasting marriage decision-making processes support this theory. Rati's father's marriage was definitely uncommon in a time when returning to India to marry was the prevalent custom. When it comes to educational level, however, both of Rati's parents have backgrounds similar to that of Rati's peers. After graduating from the Indian Institute of Technology, the MIT of India, her father moved to Wisconsin to pursue his second B.S. Imitating her father's thick Indian accent, she recites his immigration story as he tells it: "I had one suitcase, one briefcase, and $1,000; I did not need material things." Upon returning from a summer internship in Florida, he was introduced to Rati's mother by friends. Rati's mother was an Asian Studies major educated in Hindi and Mandarin Chinese who taught English in Asia while completing her M.A. Although at first she did not give him "the time of day," she eventually agreed to one date. They were married within a year.

Rati's grandparents were not overjoyed when Rati's father called them about his intentions to marry a Caucasian Lutheran, but they quietly accepted his marriage decision. His uncle had migrated a few years earlier and married a white woman so there was already a precedent. Although Rati's uncle and aunt lived in Maryland and visited a few times while she was growing up, her relationship with them wasn't solidified until later in life when she took it upon herself to make ties with her Indian relatives. While growing up, she was never conscious of the fact that her parents or aunt and uncle were bi-ethnic: "It just was," she says. Only after she left the diverse and cosmopolitan environment her university hometown provided her and her family did that consciousness emerge.

Much of Rati's adoption of an Indian identity and Hinduism later in life stems, she theorizes, from being the eldest child in her family and having visited India when she was two years old. "I don't remember that trip, but we had lots of pictures from it and I had mementos so I always asked questions about India and wanted to visit again," she explains. Her younger siblings, by contrast, lacked curiosity about their father's homeland. Rati's father, she says, was "more of a F.O.B. [than later when her younger siblings were born] so it rubbed off on me" (F.O.B. stands for "Fresh Off the Boat"; it is a derogatory term used to describe recent immigrants). Rati, unlike her siblings, knew the names and approximate times Hindu holidays fell in the year although her family celebrated only Easter and Christmas. "It's as if I was raised somewhere else [from my siblings] in a lot of ways," she concludes.

Rati describes her exposure to Indian culture while growing up as both exciting and interesting. She loved listening to her father's old Indian records and would play them in the basement. She looked forward to the rare instances when her father cooked pakoras and dosas, popular potato-based South Indian dishes, for his family. She "lived for" these surfacings of Indian identity "because it was something different." However, aside from a few Mughal-style paintings and heavily beaded pillow covers, there was no regular presence of Indian culture in her childhood home. Why? Because her father was deeply ambivalent about his roots, and there weren't other Indians in their community "to help perpetuate Indian culture."

Although Rati and her siblings had a mostly generic American upbringing (collecting Cabbage Patch Kids, watching *The Cosby Show*), when it came to dating, they were subject to strict rules. Rati, like other women and men I interviewed, dated behind her parents' backs. Her parents would often butt heads when Rati's mother defended Rati's decision to go out late at night with a mixed crowd of boys and girls. Behind his back, Rati and her siblings called their father "The Warden." He was "fearful of [dating] and disliked anything that made him feel uncomfortable," she says. "He was really strict back then."

Upon graduating from college in Texas where she studied acoustics and audio, Rati worked in post-production and talent booking in Austin, Atlanta and Urbana-Champaign. Then, as she describes it, she "came back around full circle." For years she had been exchanging Christmas cards with her aunt and uncle in Maryland. They had visited India two years prior and showed her the video they made there; instantly her interest in India was kindled. "It occurred to me that I was independent and making money and I didn't have to ask anybody permission to visit India," she says. So she started planning a trip.

Rati lived in various relatives' houses during the course of her month-long stay in India. As she puts it, "It was as if I had been there the whole time. It was as if I hadn't been gone for twenty-five years. It suddenly came together." She describes herself as religious "only for the cultural aspect not so much for the religious reasons," but, along with her extended family, she attended temple on numerous occasions during the month. She now has religious objects in her house, including mini-statues of the goddess Lakshmi and prints of the god Ganesh, but to her these images mostly signify her ties to India rather than to Hinduism.

Rati's trip to India was a catalyst in a series of events that resulted in her meeting her husband through Indian personal ads and marrying him only a few months after their first meeting. Immediately prior to her trip her parents divorced. Rati describes the divorce as "not pretty" and "uglier than it had to be." The divorce and the trip to India "changed everything for me." Perhaps more than she is willing to admit, her parents' divorce lent a hand in instigating her "return" to India in search of a more stable family to replace her newly fractured nuclear family. As she met extended family members in India and as she searched for an Indian-Hindu husband, Rati was looking for a new family.

Rati broke up with Paul, her white boyfriend, shortly after returning from her trip to India. She then began her mission to find a husband through "arranged meetings" via a matrimonial website exclusively for Indians. Culturally invigorated by her trip, Rati describes how "all this knowledge about India was something new to me and I wanted to learn more about it." Newly single and adamant that she not waste any more time dating white American men who might mistake her love of Indian culture for racism, Rati drew up a "mile-long list" of criteria she sought in a marital candidate. She then proceeded to go on-line and research various Internet matrimonial websites before posting her profile on shaadi.com.

Rati concedes that she does not think pre-modern, traditional arranged marriage is "as barbaric as Americans think it is" although she understands how the "American belief in free will" contradicts the institution of arranged marriage. She describes how when she was younger she was "more interested in whether [a date] was cool or not rather than does he have a job. When you're young you don't see in the long term; you are not necessarily the best at picking a life partner. Family involvement and advice of elders makes marriage better." When I asked her what kinds of qualities she looked for in a potential partner she describes how she was looking for someone who could provide the strong Indian cultural background that she lacked. She wanted to marry someone with a solid knowledge of Indian culture so she could learn from him and make her somewhat shaky foundation more solid. She sought a mate who could further educate her about Indian culture even as he reinforced her own ethnic-American identity.

After outlining these criteria in her matrimonial advertisement, and admitting that she drinks occasionally and has modern parents, Rati also posted a photograph of herself in a sari. She tells me how she received a response from a man in Thailand who was fluent in six languages and planning to move to the United States. She thought he was promising until, a few long-distance phone calls into their courtship, he called her "ji," a suffix meant as a formal sign of respect. She promptly dissolved that "relationship."

As if applying for a job, Shiv, Rati's future husband, sent a competitive bio-data, or resume, to Rati in response to her picture and profile on shaadi.com. Bio-datas are less popular now than they were fifteen years ago, but they remain an important component in matchmaking among conservative Indians. A typical bio-data states educational background, professional experience and even salary details not only for the candidate but also for close family members such as the parents and siblings. After first talking on the phone for three and a half hours, Rati and Shiv began having regular phone conversations before she visited him in New York. After her first visit, they began seeing each other every other weekend for three months before getting engaged.

Rati describes meeting Shiv on the matrimonial website as making their re-lationship more honest and open than if they had they met in a bar or through a friend. She tells me how "all the questions you want to ask on the first date" about marriage, family, education, and salaries "you can't ask" when meeting through conventional methods but that by the time six months roll by and "you've figured out what a guy is all about, that's six months of your life wasted." As she puts it, "On shaadi.com no one is there for a booty call. No one wants to date for fun or pass time." Plus, all the uncomfortable questions regarding money and salaries are already answered in the bio-data, leaving the boy and girl more time and energy to focus on discovering whether the two have chemistry and are compatible for mar-riage. Rati and Shiv's families were from the same region in India and belonged to the same caste, two criteria that lead Shiv to Rati's advertisement through the click of a few scroll-down menus. Having pre-determined that they were compat-ible in terms of region and caste, the two were free to pursue an American-style romance. But, as Rati describes it, "The elders could not have done a better job putting the two of us together."

Rati engaged in two models of marriage, the arranged one as well as the love one, in her arranged meeting. Rather than reject either the traditional Indian or modern American models for marriage, she embraced elements from both tradi-tions in choosing a spouse. It took her parents' divorce and her trip to India to move Rati to express her Indianness and thereby her Americanness. Rati claimed her Indian heritage upon returning from India and married Shiv to reinforce her ethnic-American identity.

Whereas Shiv and Rati's courtship began with Shiv's response to Rati's on-line matrimonial advertisement, Hamsa and Nalin met through friends while students at the University of Wisconsin. Nonetheless, Hamsa and Nalin's story (like Shiv and Rati's) emphasizes the significance among second-generation Indian-American Hindus of finding not only a co-ethnic marriage partner but also a spouse who carries a certain level of knowledge of Indian culture and Hinduism.

Like Rati and Shiv's home which contains numerous images of such gods as Krishna and Lakshmi, Hamsa's bedroom has a distinctly South-Asian aesthetic. The walls are painted a deep maroon, the dresser and night tables are made of a heavy, dark wood, and a golden statue of Ganesh sits on the windowsill over-looking the Hudson River and Manhattan's skyline. A vividly-painted image of what seems like a Moghul emperor sits framed on the dresser. The massive bed is covered with an intricately gold-bordered red comforter and five matching pillows of various sizes. Whereas the interior design is reminiscent of a maharaja's inner sanctuary, Hamsa and Nalin's wedding photographs lend the room a Bollywood feel.

Mounted above the bed are two wooden-framed photographs of the couple in traditional Indian garb. The heaviness of Hamsa's sari betrays that they are the couple's wedding portraits. However, rather than pose in traditional Indian wedding postures, which would typically feature the bride and groom standing solemnly side by side without holding hands, the poses Hamsa and Nalin strike are of a new India: modernized and westernized Bollywood. In one photograph, Hamsa sits with her chin in one palm while Nalin stands behind her hugging his hands around her neck. In another the two playfully hold hands and stand across from one another as if they are about to whirl in circles. Rather than look demure, as Indian tradition would dictate, Hamsa smiles like a love struck Bollywood ac-tress and Nalin looks like a young Amitabh Bachan (one of Bollywood's most famous actors).

Hamsa is embarrassed when I comment on how much I enjoy looking at her wedding portraits. "Yes, well we did whatever our Indian wedding photographer told us," she says. "Those poses aren't natural to us, but they're typical Indian wedding poses." What intrigues me in my conversations with Hamsa and Nalin is their inability to distinguish modernized India from the India they have configured for themselves in their imaginations. To them, India is one homogenous country with one homogenous tradition. This confession is even more striking for me because Hamsa and Nalin are a regionally mixed couple. Nalin's family is from Gujarat in Western India, and Hamsa from Andhra Pradesh in South India yet they consistently ignore the diversity of cultures within the country and remain ignorant that their own "traditional South Indian" wedding was a hybrid one.

Ironically, Hamsa and Nalin's "pure Indian-Hindu" wedding reveals how there is no pure "India." As the couple's wedding attests, India is made up of many different regional cultures and a myriad of religious faiths and languages.

Nalin was not the first Gujarati North Indian man Hamsa dated either. She tells me that although she had many friends in her ethnically diverse high school, she did not date until she arrived at college. "I had one two-month long relationship with a Gujarati Indian guy before I met Nalin," she tells me. But apparently he wasn't Indian enough:

> He was very different from Nalin. My ex-boyfriend wasn't very knowledgeable of his background, and he didn't have an Indian community growing up in West Virginia; he wasn't familiar with the religion and didn't know the language. He'd never been to India. That's why I didn't connect with that guy. He was very apathetic about being Indian.

Knowing about India was something Hamsa actively looked for in a partner. Like Nalin, she wanted to find a partner she could love but who could also assert his "Indianness," thereby reinforcing her own symbolic ethnic Indian capital, and in the process her own Americanness. She wanted to marry a man knowledgeable of his Indian-Hindu background to reflect her own cultural and religious ties with India. While outsiders might posit that Hamsa's wish to exclusively date Indians depletes her American symbolic ethnic capital, I argue that it instead makes her more American.

Nalin reports he was very intentional about exclusively dating and marrying Indian women:

> From the very beginning I always knew I would meet all types of people, but in terms of marriage I wanted to marry someone with the same cultural values. It would be easier and we would get along better. Around high school I made that choice when I started seriously thinking about dating and figuring out what I was looking for.

When asked what values are specific to Indian Hindus, he recognizes that "values" are found across cultures and re-formulates his thoughts. "It was more cultural, going to temple. Growing up, I think Indian culture brought about family closeness; family came first. In college I never thought about dating a non-Indian." When asked whether his parents were upset that he married a non-Gujarati girl, he responds, "In a perfect world I would have married a Gujarati girl, but they are educated enough to know that compatibility is more important."

During their two-year courtship at the University of Wisconsin, Hamsa and Nalin moved to San Diego for a summer where they interned and took classes. In San Diego, they tell me, they fell in love. "I didn't think I couldn't live without him," Hamsa tells me, "but I thought I would be sad if he ever left." Hamsa presses her two index fingers into her fluffy comforter and they travel, making an upside down V, until they meet at the same point. "That's how we were; we started off in different places and spent enough time together dating that we pulled each other in the same direction," she explains. For her, love for her husband was not love at first sight, but still conformed in a way to the traditional Indian view of love where one *marries first* and later grows to love one's spouse. For Hamsa, a couple *dates* and then grows to love one another.

When asked whether Hamsa's parents expected her to partake in widespread Indian-American dating rituals such as advertising in the matrimonial section of *India Abroad* or meeting eligible bachelors through an extensive family network, she responds that her parents had always wanted her to find her own partner. She describes how during their first two years of dating, her parents referred to Nalin as "her friend" when he called. Hamsa thought it was best that "through casual conversation they would find out about him. Gradually, I let them know about him little by little."

As is often the case in Indian households, Hamsa and her parents communicated their own feelings toward finding an appropriate marriage partner by indirectly talking about other people. "I had a cousin who was a little bit older than me who was having a hard time getting married," Hamsa tells me. "They were afraid that that would happen to me as well. It was more in discussions about my older cousins that my parents would express their views on dating and marrying. They would say things like, 'She never dated, she never looked and all of a sudden she's twenty-eight and picky about whom she wants to marry.'" Through conversations about their nieces and nephews, Hamsa's parents conveyed to Hamsa that "you can't start too late, but don't want to start too early, and it's important to start to look on your own." Likewise, Nalin had decided that he "wanted to do it myself. I knew that if I didn't do it myself that I would have to use other means to meet someone, and I firmly believe that meeting people through your friends is the best way because they know you two the best."

Neither Hamsa nor Nalin resorted to publishing a matrimonial ad, but they purposefully sought to date Hindu Indians. Hamsa's Gujarati ex-boyfriend was not Indian enough; he was not as curious about Indian culture as Nalin, nor did he place as much emphasis on what Nalin describes as "Indian cultural values." While still in high school, Nalin decided to marry an Indian. And their collective pride for their ethnic heritage is demonstrated in Nalin and Hamsa's wedding day festivities.

Intent on having as Indian a wedding as possible and on distancing themselves from the mainstream white American weddings they associated with white Christians and Jews, both of the featured couples in this chapter, Rati and Shiv and Hamsa and Nalin, demonstrate ethnic American identities, their Americanness as well as their Indianness. In the following sections of "The Marriage Market," I focus on themes that resonate in the stories of how Rati and Shiv and Hamsa and Nalin met. These themes dominated my interviews with other couples and betray the delicate balance of disclosure and secrecy immigrant parents and second-generation Indian-American Hindus face when negotiating the marriage market.

Factors in Marrying a Co-Ethnic

The couples whom I met and interviewed were eager to share with me their stories. But so were extended family members, friends of friends, first-generation Indian immigrant parents, and perfect strangers who learned I was researching weddings among second-generation Indian-American Hindus. Clearly, marriage is a significant topic of discussion among first- and second-generation Indian-American Hindus.

Given the emphasis on endogamy, on marrying inside their community, I wondered why or whether this approach sparked any concerns that the second-generation Americans might be viewed as separatist or racist by the larger community in which they live. Unfortuantely, a dearth of scholarship regarding American attitudes toward South Asians mirrors the lack of dialogue around this difficult subject in my interviews with second-generation Indian-American Hindus. Second-generation Indian-American Hindus do not engage in conversations regarding their racial and ethnographic status. This may be because of their socio-economically elevated status in mainstream American society. Perhaps my participants' advantaged backgrounds shield them from discussions about race. Vijay Prashad's *The Karma of Brown Folk* (2000) analyzes Indians' lack of political and racial awareness. It also describes the first and second generations' distance from minorities such as blacks and Hispanics, making it one of the few full works on racism towards and among Indian Americans. Prashad posits that Indian-Americans and their immigrants distance themselves from issues of race because they see themselves as "exempt" of such concerns since Indians are widely respected in mainstream America as a "model minority." In *The Karma of Brown Folk*, Prashad suggests the Indian-immigrant and second-generation Indian-American communities need to engage more deeply with minority groups such as blacks and Hispanics and confront issues of race in American politics.

Although religion works as a method to indoctrinate Indian-American Hindus into developing an ethnic-American identity, it does not differentiate themselves significantly from their peers or even consciously connect them to like-minded Hindus. Instead, religion works more subversively. Rather than worshipping the same deities or subscribing to the same religious stories, it is everyday worship (for example, doing aarti, or offering homage to a deity, and offering prasad, sweet kernels of sugar) that serves as a connecting force between second-generation Indian-American Hindus.

More than Hindu beliefs, Hindu practices and the intimacies associated with them are what distinguish Indian-American Hindus who have symbolic ethnic Indian capital from those who do not. Knowing the story of how Ganesh got his elephant head is not as important as knowing how to place fruit in front of a deity or knowing to bring one's forehead and hands to the base of a statue when in prayer. This physical intimacy, a central feature of Hindu religious rituals, contributes to one's value on the marriage market far more than an encyclopedic knowledge "outsiders" may gain from studying Hinduism in America. Moreover, this practical, ritual knowledge becomes especially valuable at the wedding ceremony.

For the second generation, "being Indian" does not just require having immigrant Hindu parents from India; it also includes having an Indian-American identity. Activities such as attending temple or having Indian "weekend friends" are essential in nurturing an Indian-American identity. Despite the fact that Hinduism does not have much of a presence in the daily lives of the second-generation Indian-Hindu Americans I met, attending temple and performing religious rituals create shared experiences that link second-generation Americans to one another and distinguish those who have symbolic ethnic Indian capital from those who do not.[1] Intimacy with the simple rituals associated with Rakhi, a Hindu holiday that celebrates the bond between female and male siblings, is valued in part because it distinguishes those who have been consciously raised as Indian-American Hindus from those who have not. Marrying someone who has this knowledge also ensures that these rituals and practices will live in the next generation.

Belonging to a Hindu religious or Indian cultural organization was another important shared experience among the second-generation Indian-American Hindus I interviewed. Many of the men and women I met participated in religious or cultural clubs in college, but none of them found these organizations useful in meeting a potential spouse and all of them outgrew these associations after graduation. However, while students at university, nearly all the second-generation Indian-American Hindus I met belonged to organizations such as New York University's Shruti, a secular cultural group for students of South Asian ethnic heritage. Many of the men and women I met were members of the Network of Indian Professionals, a national organization sociologist Nazli Kibria describes "as important to the maintenance and expression of Indianness, or ethnic identity as Indian American." [2]

Indian-American Hindus were for the most part attracted to fellow Indians who could symbolically express their Indianness via membership in a cultural or religious organization. Belonging to a religious or cultural organization does not directly lead to finding a marriage partner yet membership to one increases one's chance of marrying an Indian-American Hindu.

Negative qualities of Indian culture such as its patriarchal culture were for the most part ignored in my conversations with second-generation Indian-American Hindus who selectively integrated "positive" aspects of the culture (yoga, bhangra dance, Bollywood films and Indian food) into their lives. Just like Vijay Prashad notes how Indian Americans don't generally engage in socially-conscious political debates because they are members of a "model minority," they do not openly discuss the gender division or misogyny in Indian families. Perhaps in an effort to protect their reputation as members of a model minority, first-generation Indian-American Hindus refrain from critically examining their society and culture.

www.Shaadi.com: Where Buds of Romance Bloom on the Internet

Far more than cultural and religious groups, the Internet played a big matchmaking role among the men and women I interviewed. In fact, twenty-five percent of my study's participants met via Internet matrimonial ads or dabbled in online dating prior to meeting their spouse. Second-generation Americans and their immigrant parents appreciate websites such as shaadi.com where one can search for prospective Hindu Indians and Indian Americans with compatible personality traits and lifestyles. The drop-down menus on shaadi.com require that the "boy" or "girl" choose the Indian dialect their family speaks, the region in India their family originates from, and the religious sect their family belongs to. Although parents and extended family members usually lead the search when using newspaper matrimonial ads, the technology behind the Internet has intimidated many of these meddling family members to rely on their sons and daughters to search for a spouse on their own. Unmarried Indian-American men and women are often described as "boys" and "girls," indicating their infantilization despite their age, maturity, level of education and professional success. On the Internet, those seeking a match can filter out candidates right away based on these drop-down menus, ensuring that they only meet candidates with the same linguistic, ethnic and religious background, which is to say the sort of background that would meet the approval of parents and grandparents.

At this point the "American" portion of the spousal selection process begins. The web surfer reads the mandatory "describe yourself" text box that includes a list of hobbies, a physical description, and an outline of what one is looking for in a soul mate. The search for a potential marriage partner shifts at this key point from traditionally Indian to traditionally American, supporting my overarching thesis that the Indian-Hindu community's desire for second-generation Indian-American Hindus to marry peers who express both an ethnic and an American identity is reflected in both the arranged meeting model for dating and the wedding day.

Rati's story describes a second-generation American's search for a spouse whose ethnic identity would reinforce her own. It also illustrates the significance of the Internet in allowing Indian-American Hindus to play matchmaker for themselves and create relationships that span the globe. Jennifer Egan's *New York Times* article about Internet dating, "Love in the Time of No Time," does not specifically refer to ethnic websites such as shaadi.com, but it does discuss the significance that financial stability and affluence, two significant criteria in the search for a spouse in the Indian-American Hindu community, have in meeting potential partners. One of Rati's reasons for using shaadi.com was so she could have the financial and practical information she needed upfront. Egan argues, "There is nothing new about the idea of marriage as a business transaction. Online dating is not the opposite of this [romantic] approach to love, but its radical extension."[3] In some ways, online dating among mainstream Americans looking for a spouse on match.com is no different from online dating among people like Rati and Shiv who meet on shaadi.com: significant practical details such as faith, occupation and lifestyle are disclosed upfront on one's profile so that potential partners can determine if they are compatible or not. Although Rati did not have specific ideas about how money much her ideal spouse should ideally earn, she was focused on finding a man with a stable job with earning potential.

Three characteristics immediately present themselves on shaadi.com. First, shaadi.com personal ads are almost always submitted by the marital candidates themselves rather than by family members. In creating a profile, the spouse seeker has to answer if she is designing her own profile. She is then asked to write two paragraphs of one hundred words or more describing her family and what she is looking for in a partner. So while family has by no means disappeared in this high-tech view, singles are searching for a marital partner on their own; they are (relatively) free agents in their own search for a spouse.

A second characteristic is the preponderance of personal ads that focus on interests, hobbies, and activities. In creating one's profile on shaadi.com, a marital candidate can quickly chose from a drop-down menu the religions, sects, geographic areas and ranges of complexion they are looking for in a spouse (complexions range from fair to wheatish to dark). These drop-downs leave room in the text box to get creative and distinguish one's ads from the thousands of others.

One New York resident, Neelu1107, writes,

> Nutty. Mostly smooth with a few rough spots. Seemingly malleable, but harder to shake about than suspected. Kind of like peanut butter. To be more specific, I'm a 2nd year law student trapped in a 25 year old body. Mentally, I'm about 12:). On the hunt for a fellow pre-teen trapped in adult form to share a never-ending adolescence with:).
>
> Hopefully You Are: Vibrant. Sweet with a little sour zing. Mostly got it together, yet able to break it down. Kind of like jelly.
>
> P. S. This may come off as rather female dog like but if you're still confused about the direction of your life, if you feel like you need to explore the world alone, if you feel like there is so much more you need to accomplish/wrap up in your life before you get into something serious, if you feel like you need to casually date for months and months on end, I am NOT the person for you. I guess my profile is deceiving in that sense and seems very casual. For all those who weren't totally scared off by the last few sentences, I look forward to getting to know you :)

Neelu1107 takes a risky approach for finding a serious life partner by writing in commonplace metaphors such as "peanut butter" and "jelly." But she makes it plain that she is on a search for a serious relationship. Like Rati, she says she does not want to "casually date for months and months on end."

Finally, shaadi.com's personal ads epitomize the diasporic reality Indian Hindus now inhabit. Rather than limit themselves to meeting like-minded locals, profiles on shaadi.com more often than not indicate that the men and women using this site are open to meeting people in Southeast Asia, India, the United States, Canada, and England. For example, Rati's first serious beau on shaadi.com lived in Singapore. There is something of a U.S. bias on the site, however. Often, singles looking for a partner on shaadi.com indicate their preference for a spouse with permanent residency in the United States. Frequently, non-U.S. citizens use the transnational Indian-Hindu marriage market to fulfill their more self-centered goals such as moving to America. A common story concerns the foreigner who marries an American for a green card.

India Abroad

Before the advent of the Internet and websites like shaadi.com, the most widespread method of organizing an arranged meeting was by placing a matrimonial advertisement in the nationally read newspaper *India Abroad*. Sociologist Madhulika

Khandelwal describes *India Abroad* as founded in 1970 in New York City by professionals who immigrated from India post-1965 and whose main goal was to cultivate a network for fellow NRIs (non-resident Indians). Over the years the space provided for matrimonial advertisements has expanded, making it the oldest resource for matchmaking among Indians in India and abroad.

Publishing a matrimonial ad in newspapers like *India Abroad* was perceived by my participants as an outdated method for making an arranged meeting. In fact, none of the couples I met posted ads in *India Abroad* or other old-fashioned paper periodicals. The second generation relies on the Internet more than print periodicals for their news which is one reason why the Internet is a popular venue for matchmaking. Another financially practical reason is that the cost per word to publish an ad in the newspaper makes it more expensive than registering for free on an Internet website where advertisers pay for the website's maintenance through the publishing of ads. Additionally, on the Internet a spouse-seeker can quickly use drop-down menus to describe in detail one's ethnic and religious background, and few employ the text box as a space to make the ad more personal. The fee per word for publishing a matrimonial ad in a newspaper leaves little if any room to describe the prospective marriage candidate beyond describing his or her regional, religious and education background.

Although the Internet is replacing the matrimonial ads of *India Abroad*, looking at the newspaper may shed some light on the seemingly contradictory yet successfully compromised values both Indian immigrants and second-generation Indian-American Hindus look for in a spouse. For the vast majority of the participants, early memories of reading the matrimonial advertisements in *India Abroad* served as their first exposure to the Indian marriage market. Even as early as thirteen or fourteen years of age, participants found themselves engrossed in the descriptive profiles in the concluding pages of the newspaper. This was the first time many of my participants were aware of the marriage market they would one day consider as a means to meet their future spouse.

Newspaper matrimonial ads in *India Abroad* demonstrate how selection criteria have evolved over time. Whereas being a Hindu and ethnically Indian remain important to the first generation, sharing the same language and originating from the same region of India have lost much of their significance in the last five to ten years. First-generation Indian Americans are now more open to marrying their daughters and sons to people whose families come from different regions of India and speak a different language. Reportedly less tied to these traditional criteria, Indian parents are more focused on finding a son- or daughter-in-law with equal or better educational and/or professional qualifications than themselves.

The immigrant generation is most concerned with their son or daughter marrying someone with financial security and education. This is especially evident in newspaper advertisements placed by families who rank high on the socioeconomic ladder. Class, in other words, plays not only a definitive role in determining how much importance a family placed on regional background, but also an obvious one.

Although second-generation Americans normally utilize the Internet rather than printed periodicals in seeking a mate, the second-generation Indian-American

Hindus who do submit ads to newspapers such as *India Abroad* are revolutionizing these traditionally conservative advertisements. These newspaper personal ads read more and more like the profiles on shaadi.com.

A typical ad in *India Abroad* is terse, to the point, and usually written by a "boy" or "girl" in India seeking a marriage partner. In short, these ads are very businesslike, sounding less like a match.com profile and more like a mail-order bride advertisement. One reason for this stiffness may be that English is not always the spouse seeker's first language. A typical *India Abroad* matrimonial ad reads like Raj Kumar's:

> There are five members in my family. Two brothers and one sister. Sister married. I like true friends. My interest is watching cricket, listening news and watching/reading Science and technology.

Because a large percentage of newspaper matrimonial ads are placed by Indian residents, it should not be surprising that none of the couples I met advertised in *India Abroad*. Whereas ten years ago immigrant parents often resorted to placing ads on behalf of their sons and daughters in *India Abroad*, parents do not place ads on matrimonial websites. However, all the second-generation Indian-American Hindus I met described the pressure imposed on them by parents eager to see their children married to someone "suitable."

Playing Marriage Broker: Parents' Involvement in their Child's Marriage

Not a single participant in my study had a parent directly involved in introducing a child to potential spouses. The first and second generation's compromise, the arranged meeting system, which embraces both traditional Indian and modern American models for marriage, is partly a result of the cross-generational realization that only through implementing both philosophies will all their destinies as Hindus be fulfilled. Fully rejecting the American model for a love marriage would only incite friction between the two generations. While most Indian-American Hindus I interviewed complained to some degree of the emphasis their parents had placed on their marrying in a timely manner, few understand the pressures on parents to marry off their children, and to marry them "well." Socially there is tremendous pressure among one's first-generation peers to have one's children married in a timely manner, but there also exists a religious mandate that parents take responsibility for marrying their sons and daughters. A parent's final duty is ensuring that his or her children marry suitably. Thereby only after that duty is fulfilled are parents free to see to their own spiritual lives and devote themselves more fully to their faith.

While marrying off one's children propels Hindu parents from the household stage of life into a stage dedicated to the pursuit of spiritual realization, marriage is also an important rite of passage for the husband and wife, who will no longer be referred as a "boy" and "girl." Marrying off one's American-Hindu child places a parent in Hinduism's third stage of life, vanprastha (retiree), in addition to permitting the second-generation newly married Hindu American to enter the second stage, grahastha (householder).

The friction between the American value of individual autonomy and the Indian value of respecting parental authority often presents itself in the Indian-American context, but discussion around marriage also brings to surface the immigrant and second-generation Indian-Hindu Americans' disparate views of adulthood. In America, mainstream ideas surrounding adulthood see marriage as a rite of passage but not a prerequisite to becoming an adult. In short, one can be an adult without being married. Becoming an adult in America hinges on turning eighteen and being considered an adult by the American legal system. American ideas concerning adulthood are closely associated with the value American culture places on both individualism and self-reliance. Whereas the law and society establish Americans as adults by eighteen years of age, notions about the significance of marriage and its role in the Hindu community suggest Hindu notions of entering adulthood are very different. The most obvious example of this difference appears repeatedly in language surrounding the Indian-Hindu marriage market when prospective marital candidates are referred to as "girls and boys" despite their age, level of education, income and profession.

However, the degree to which parents play matchmaker depends heavily on the family's socio-economic standing. In a blue-collar Indian-American community in Jackson Heights, New York, marriages are sometimes arranged, but the well-educated upper-class Indian Americans who participated in this study were agents in choosing their spouses. The higher up in the socio-economic hierarchy, the less involved parents tend to be in their child's marriage decision-making process. Only in one instance did I meet a young man whose parents were secretly seeking a match for him. He learned about this when he randomly Googled his name and found his bio-data posted online.

Secret Pleasure: Dating as Subversive

Although immigrant parents are eager to see their children married, dating remains a charged topic in the Indian-American community. In fact, it is rarely tolerated until the second-generation participants are of marriageable age. Hesitantly, immigrant parents promote dating following an arranged meeting as a pre-requisite to marriage. But a set of strict rules surround dating in the Indian-American Hindu community. Of the twenty couples I interviewed, none of the Indian-American men and women were allowed to date in high school. Sachi, a PhD candidate in Sociology at University of Pennsylvania, describes the "don't ask, don't tell" unspoken agreement between parents and their children regarding dating. Without their parents telling them that dating is forbidden, second-generation Americans somehow know better than to think dating is allowed.

Even though dating in high school and even college is a no-no among almost all Indian-American Hindus, all but one family supported dating with the intent of marriage. However, another unspoken understanding exists. While the immigrant

population supports its children in dating with the intent to marry, the second generation is not allowed to incorporate a boyfriend or girlfriend into the family circle
until the relationship is official. Like Hamsa, many participants told me how they
did not even introduce a boyfriend or girlfriend to their parents until a formal engagement could be announced. Only two couples in my sample introduced their
boyfriends or girlfriends to parents without intending to marry them in the im-
mediate to near future. More often than not, second-generation Indian-American
Hindus date secretly for months or even years before introducing a boyfriend or
girlfriend to each other's parents.

First-generation Indians, most of them unfamiliar with the phenomenon of
dating for extended periods of time, have come to an unspoken agreement with
their daughters and sons whereby boyfriends and girlfriends are "just friends"
until an engagement is formalized. Hamsa described her boyfriend as simply a
"friend" who called often. All too often, Indian parents read any introduction
to a child's boyfriend or girlfriend as a fairly formal step immediately prior to
engagement.

Another reason why American-style disclosure is problematic for second-
generation Indian Americans is that to admit to dating is to admit that one is a
sexual being. Rather than flaunting one's blooming sexuality, Indians generally
hide it. Adult sexuality is only acceptable when one is married. While a "boy"
or a "girl," sexuality is considered dangerous and threatens the notion that unmarried Indian-American Hindus are in fact children until they marry. While dating
is more openly acceptable in India's cosmopolitan cities, in most of the country
this practice remains secret. Second-generation Indian-American Hindus prefer
hiding their path to adulthood over presenting themselves to parents and grandparents as autonomous and independent sexual adults. But sexuality cannot be
ignored forever. Tensions regarding the display of sexuality often arise on the
wedding day, not least with the bride's choice of wedding apparel, which in the
American context is typically a telling symbol of sexuality on display.

Just as the mediating model for arranged meetings has been negotiated ahead
of time, a commonly agreed upon method for discussing (and not discussing)
marriage also exists. All my participants were acquainted with the marriage discussions Hamsa had with her parents. Rather than speaking in a straightforward
manner about what Hamsa should look for in a marriage partner, Hamsa's parents tiptoed around the subject by discussing Hamsa's cousin. Rather than warn
Hamsa against waiting too long to marry, her parents discussed her older cousin
who was struggling to marry well. As a way of giving Hamsa "permission" to
date and find a partner on her own, they told Hamsa how her cousin was alone
at twenty-eight because she "never dated." Observing Hamsa's cousin's parents
futile attempts to introduce their daughter to eligible young men, Hamsa's parents
opted out of helping Hamsa find a spouse and instead told her to start looking on
her own time. But even Hamsa's parents did not want dating details. Even they
observed the "don't ask, don't tell" compromise.

This "don't ask, don't tell" approach is standard during dating. But indirect-
ness yields to directness on the wedding day. Unabashedly and proudly, Nalin and
Hamsa announced their long courtship to their extended families and friends at

their wedding reception by showing a slide show of photographs from their years of dating at the University of Wisconsin. Whereas some guests were probably surprised, most guests were acquainted with the fact that many long relationships do not surface until the day of the wedding. A recurring theme was how few people knew their niece or nephew, cousin or family friend is involved in a longstanding relationship before the wedding. At the wedding, however, the secret is revealed and all is forgiven. A college friend or colleague from work recounts an anecdote from the couple's courtship or a sibling shows a slide show of the happy couple. Rather than expressing anger at being kept in the dark, older family members and friends are usually pleased with the fact that the couple has remained discreet. Moreover, keeping this secret is typically understood as a sign of respect, not of dissembling. In the end, everyone is happy: the young couple revels in the companionship that comes from a long dating relationship and their parents are secretly relieved that they have been spared both the responsibility of finding a spouse for their son or daughter and the details of their premarital sexual lives.

Prejudice in the Indian-American Hindu Community

The second-generation Indian-American Hindus I met were, across the board, sensitive and embarrassed by their parents' prejudices, both racial and religious. Unlike the first generation's relatively hands-off policy towards dating, immigrant parents have no qualms about voicing their disapproval of marrying an African American or Muslim. Whereas many of the women and men I met confessed to dating in secret, all but two women admitted that, although they were open to engaging in serious relationships with Indians and whites, they were not open to such relationships with Muslims or blacks. According to Sapna, when two of her Indian-American friends married white Americans her friends' families were initially upset but eventually "adjusted." However, Sapna adds, "there were some things my parents were not okay with," including one friend's brother's decision to marry an African-American woman. Although Sapna's mother said it was okay for their family friends, it was "not okay for us." Sapna continues: "Clearly nobody has married a Muslim. Even though our views our different, our parents' views are like their parents."

The women and men I met unanimously agreed that marrying a Muslim was out of the question based on their parents' ingrained biases against Muslims. Often the men and women I met described a strong "Hindu-Muslim divide." While Hindu Americans disapprove of marrying Muslims because it would incur their parents' wrath, they may also distance themselves from Muslim Americans as a way of avoiding Muslim stigmatization in the United States post 9/11.

Many participants recall listening as children to their parents' fury with Mira Nair's film *Mississippi Masala* (1991), which depicts a relationship between a Uganda-raised Indian woman and her African-American boyfriend, played by Denzel Washington. The immigrant population in America criticized Nair's movie for depicting Indians as racist. But many of my second-generation participants also recall their parents' queasiness towards a movie about an Indian woman in love with a black man. Nair's heroine, Mina, is interesting in that she is not an Indian American struggling to establish her Indianness or Americanness. Instead, she is "masala," a term commonly used to describe a mix of spices for Indian dishes. More specifically, she is an Indian woman whose family lived in Africa for generations before moving to the American South where she meets Denzel Washington's character.

The second generation justified what might be interpreted as its racism by interpreting dating or marrying an African American as a rejection of Indian family values and a purposeful dismissal of Indian culture. Engaging in a relationship with a Muslim is also thought of as relinquishing all ties with the Indian-Hindu community. The participants in this study spent much time discussing the impossibility of marrying a Muslim despite the fact that they met Muslim Americans in their graduate programs as well as in the workplace. A black man or woman's skin color immediately distinguishes him or herself whereas Muslim Southeast Asians blend into the Southeast Asian community. There are no physically defining characteristics that distinguish a Hindu from a Muslim except for a kufi skull cap. However, in reverence to their parents' wishes (and in fear of their wrath), none of the Indian-Hindu Americans I spoke with were willing at any point to pursue a relationship with a Muslim.

"Returning" to the Home Land to Marry

Another common theme in conversations Indian-American Hindu women had with their parents was caution towards marrying an Indian national. In fact, the women I met were often reproached by their parents for dating an Indian national. Whereas the musical band Apache Indians in their song "Arranged Marriage" admit how they want to return to India to find a prototypical Indian wife who will properly cook them roti (Indian bread), only three out of the twenty women I interviewed for this book married men from India, and none of the men I interviewed married women from India. The common stereotype is for a second-generation Indian-American Hindu man to "return" to India to find a wife after years of serial dating and premarital sex with white and Indian-American women alike. However, my research indicates that Indian-American Hindu women are more likely to marry an Indian.

Much debate exists among second-generation Indian-American Hindus regarding whether they should marry people from India as opposed to America. Sociologist Johanna Lessinger writes that:

> Women, with their American-bred sense of independence, tend to prefer young men raised, like themselves, in the U.S. They know that men from India will demand a kind of service and subservience they are not prepared to give. Many also complain that Indian men are shy, poorly dressed, awkward and unsure in American social situations. [4]

In my study, however, whereas none of the men I met married a woman Indian born and raised, fifteen percent of the women I met married a man from the subcontinent. Whereas Lessinger's subjects, blue-collar women who live in Jackson Heights, feared marrying traditional, lower-class Indian men from India, the women I met were considering (and in some cases marrying) progressive, sophisticated men from the subcontinent. However, none of the men I met admitted to seeking a docile Indian wife, and none visited India to find a spouse.

Sapna's mother rejected the idea of her American-born-and-raised daughter marrying Satish, Sapna's Indian-born-and raised boyfriend. "For a few months I kept dropping hints to my mom about how I was talking to a guy at work," Sapna says. "She knew he was Indian from India and kept blowing it off because she was worried that he might be too conservative; she hoped that it would go away." Sapna's mother had heard about unhappy marriages between American-raised women and Indian-raised men and knew her daughter would never make a typical Indian wife. Household chores and cooking were not Sapna's top priorities or talents, and her mother was afraid that a culture clash might arise if her daughter married an Indian man. After months of ignoring the seriousness of her daughter's relationship with Satish, Sapna put her foot down and told her parents that they would have to meet him. "It took some time for them to get used to each other," Sapna recalls. "It took four or five months. They didn't click right away." Sapna cited Satish's fluency with Hindi and his comfort level with traveling through India as reasons why she felt herself attracted to him. She also valued his intimate knowledge of Indian history and his ability to cook Indian food, since both skills compensated for her own ignorance and would come in handy when it was time to have a family.

Although the Indian-American women in this study who married men from India did so willingly, sometimes marriage to an Indian man from India served as a threat. Saijala describes how she and her father butted heads on a regular basis in her adolescent and young adulthood years. During an angry fight, Sachi's father threatened to "marry me off to someone from India who could keep me in line." The only instance in Saijala's life where arranged marriage was suggested was in a fit of anger and served as a threat to subdue her stubborn ways. This threat is indicative of the larger Indian American community's stereotype of Indian-born men and American-born women and the incompatibility of the two in marriage.

Conclusion

Second-generation Indian-American Hindus, in keeping with their parents' wishes, prefer to marry a fellow Hindu who shared their Indian heritage. But this generation differs from their parents' generation in one important way. Among second-generation Indian-American Hindus, a third model for marriage holds sway. Arranged meetings, as I call this model, is a compromise already reached by the immigrant and second generations whereby young Indian-American Hindus combine traditional Indian and modern American models of marriage. Rather than choosing between the love marriage and arranged marriage, the second generation dates and chooses its spouses. It does so, however, by selectively screening out candidates who would not be acceptable to the prior generation.

On-line matrimonial sites and networks are the most popular methods for making an arranged meeting; placing an ad in a newspaper is now considered old school. Five couples in this study met through their networks of family and friends while another five met through matrimonial websites on the Internet or dabbled in dating via on-line matrimonial ads prior to meeting their spouses.

The search for a spouse was often complicated by the desire to find an Indian-American Hindu who is well educated, earns a respectable salary, and acts, thinks, and speaks in ways that other Indians perceive as Indian. Symbolic ethnic Indian and American capital are not traits one can highlight in a drop-down menu on shaadi.com, but evidence of these criteria are everywhere. In this study, claiming to love Bollywood films and owning an apartment in Manhattan, inserting Hindi metaphors in every day conversation and starting a hedge fund, are combinations of characteristics that attract second-generation Hindus and their immigrant parents.

One surprising finding of this study is that second-generation Indian-American Hindus articulate their Americanness when they articulate their Indianness. Being Indian, in other words, is not incompatible with being an American. Choosing an Indian spouse reinforces one's ethnicity while simultaneously expressing one's Americanness. In short, my participants embraced their ethnic heritage as a way to assert their Americanness rather than detract from it. Indianness, like Hinduness, is socially acceptable in the United States. More than that, however, it is actually desirable. Second-generation Indian Americans select future spouses who exhibit Indianness as a way to integrate into America rather than as a way to opt out.

Finally, it is important to note that the point in which the participants in my study got engaged was in itself a ritual that set the tone for both families' involvement in planning the wedding. Examining the various ways in which second-generation Indian-American Hindus come to the decision to marry and the methods they choose for getting engaged sheds light on how they negotiate values (such as obeying parental authority) handed down by their Indian immigrant parents. Respecting both Indian and American tradition becomes tricky during the engagement stage when second-generation Indian Americans embrace both the mainstream American engagement ritual of proposing privately with a diamond ring and the far more public Hindu engagement tradition.

Notes

1. Fiction writer Jhumpa Lahiri chronicles the childhood of Gogol Ganguli, the second-generation Indian-American hero in the novel *The Namesake*, whose immigrant parents create a distinctly Indian home life despite living in a culturally and ethnically homogeneous Massachusetts suburb.

2. Nazli Kibria, "South Asian Americans," in *Asian Americans: Contemporary Trends and Issues*, ed. Pyong Gap Min (CA: Sage Publications, 2005), 218.

3. Jennifer Egan, "Love in the Time of No Time," *New York Times*, 23

November 2003, 68.

4. Johanna Lessinger, *From the Ganges to the Hudson: Indian Immigrants in New York City* (Boston: Allyn and Bacon, 1995), 123.

The Engagement Proposal: To Dower or To Diamond?

Upon graduating from the University of Wisconsin, Hamsa and Nalin moved to New York where they began their professional lives. Finally, after dating for three years, the couple decided to introduce each other and their families to one another. During lunch at Hamsa's parents' home, Nalin's father announced, "You two have been dating for three years; we think you should get married. You should stop dating and get engaged." Hamsa's mother joined in, fearful that if her daughter and Nalin broke up, Hamsa would "have to start all over again." Nalin's parents, on the other hand, had "moral issues with dating and thought dating for a long time was a bad thing." The couple was having pre-marital sex, as Nalin's parents had correctly guessed, and Nalin's family was what Nalin describes as:

> Ideological about it; my parents think, "You meet someone, like them, and then marry. You don't date for years." I thought having premarital sex was normal and healthy. I felt guilty when I was younger, but after a while I knew it was the right thing. This is a decision you're going to be in for the rest of your life.

Nalin proposed six months later with a diamond engagement ring at a park outside the Swaminarayan Temple in Weehawken, New Jersey. Hamsa tells me:

> We went to the temple afterwards and prayed for five minutes. It was a nice way to start our engagement. We had been to temple with his parents before, but never alone. That's why he picked that spot, because the temple is there.

Never having attended temple without their parents, Hamsa and Nalin took it upon themselves to worship together as they made their first step towards adulthood.

In this chapter, I focus on four couples' stories to illustrate dominant trends for getting engaged among second-generation Indian-American Hindus. Hamsa and Nalin's engagement suggests a number of different themes in how second-generation Indian-American Hindus get engaged. First, Hamsa and Nalin's engagement proposal combined the non-religious, American tradition of spontaneously proposing with a diamond ring with the Indian-Hindu custom of praying at a significant moment in their lives. Ten out of twenty couples I interviewed had both a typically American marriage proposal with the accoutrement of a diamond ring and some sort of puja (the Hindi word for "worship"). Within the community, second-generation Indian-American Hindus are expected to participate in both the American and Indian-Hindu engagement rituals. Just as engaging in the third model for marriage, arranged meetings, integrated both the modern American notion of a love marriage with the pre-modern Indian institution of arranged marriage, the community expects young couples to participate in both the American and Indian engagement rituals.

Until the lunch with their parents, Hamsa and Nalin's relationship was a private one. However, upon introducing one another as boyfriend and girlfriend, the couple made their relationship available to their parents' criticism (or approval). Second-generation Indian-American Hindus often hide their romantic relationships from their immigrant parents; the lunch where Nalin's father said the couple should marry demonstrates why. However, rather than express annoyance, Nalin was proud of their parents' involvement: "It was an all-encompassing process with our parents. It wasn't just us getting engaged. It was a decision made jointly."

Nalin is plainly nostalgic for Indian family life where all significant decisions are made communally and with the elders' blessings. His pride in having his parents' backing with regard to marrying Hamsa highlights his desire for a close extended family and conveys respect and obedience towards the immigrant generation. Finally, Nalin and Hamsa's decision to pray after their typical American engagement proposal illustrates their identity as "occasional Hindus." Hamsa admits that whereas she and Nalin had never up until that point attended temple on their own volition, their engagement seemed like the perfect occasion to express their religious identities.

Like Nalin and Hamsa's engagement which integrated both the mainstream American and Indian-Hindu customs, Chandana and Geet's engagement also combined a private proposal with a puja. However, Chandana and Geet was the only couple I met that struggled with philosophical issues that surfaced while engaging in both sets of traditions. Chandana, in particular, was intent on avoiding conspicuous consumption in her engagement with Geet and on their wedding day. Additionally, she spoke of negotiating her family's expectations of her new role as a wife with the demands of her law career.

At first glance, Chandana looks more traditional than her second-generation Indian-American Hindu peers; she is wearing a gold and black necklace, a piece of jewelry popular among married Hindu women in India. Just like a diamond ring carries symbolic meaning in America, the mangalsutra is popular in Hindu India. The mangalsutra is a traditional gold and onyx wedding necklace that the bride wears when she marries; it takes on symbolic meaning akin to a wedding band. Chandana is the only woman I met who wears the necklace so often adorning the women of her mother's generation. However, despite this outer show of traditionalism, Chandana has a personal philosophy towards engagement and marriage that conflicted with what her parents wanted. Chandana's wedding to Geet was the only one where I witnessed a woman with feminist values and contempt for conspicuous consumption wrestle with how to plan a wedding.

Born in Albany, New York, in 1976 to Malayali-speaking, Kerala-raised physician parents, Chandana grew up in Venice, Florida, before attending Columbia University and then Yale Law School. Whereas her parents were part of a large South Asian community that revolved around attending temple, Chandana describes herself as only "nominally a part of their community." Her real Indian community was one she visited annually in India and it centered on her grandmother who tutored her in Sanskrit.

Geet, Chandana's husband, was born in Mysore in 1970 and grew up in Bombay before moving to New York in 1994 to pursue his M.B.A. in Finance and M.A. in Computer Science at New York University. Geet, despite his South Indian Brahmin upbringing (Brahmins belong to the highest and most prestigious caste in India), did not regularly attend temple during his childhood in India. Instead, he followed his father's example by doing a short daily prayer after his morning shower, a habit that fell by the wayside upon arriving in the United States.

Chandana's unorthodox attitude toward marriage left her questioning whether she would ever marry:

> For a long time I wasn't sure that I would even get married because you know marriage for a South Asian woman is often fraught with so many compromises and comes with a whole host of social expectations in the South Asian context that I wasn't sure I'd want to buy into. I knew if I was going to marry, my marriage had to be aligned with my philosophy and ideals. I didn't envision [marriage] would definitely happen for me. My parents both worked. I would see how it was often up to the wife to juggle the family and career. Within the household, dynamics really hadn't changed. Husbands aren't always supportive of their wife's ambitions. My dad's career took off while my mom made compromises. That sort of model wasn't something I wanted to replicate.

When I ask her if she ever considered dating or marrying a non-Indian because it might lessen the pressure of making the compromises she describes, she nods no, adding that the problems she saw in her parents' marriage were not unique to the community.

Whereas Chandana was open to dating non-Indian Hindus, Geet describes how he nonetheless wanted to meet someone "interested in India that had a connection with Indian culture." He confesses, "I had a bias towards marrying a South Indian despite the fact that I spent most of my years in North India and few of my friends are South Indian." In fact, he says he exclusively dated South Indian women.

The couple met during Chandana's second year of law school while she was in New York interviewing for summer clerkships. A mutual friend introduced the two with the intent of setting them up. Staying in touch via e-mail, Chandana and Geet began dating that summer when she moved to New York. Although the two had their own private engagement proposal, Chandana's parents held an engagement ceremony attended by thirty close family members and friends.

The day commenced with the women in Chandana's family holding a Ganesha puja. Geet wore a kurta (a traditional Indian man's outfit made up of loose pajama pants and a matching tunic) and later changed into one given to him as a gift by Chandana's parents. Likewise, Chandana followed tradition by changing into a sari given to her by Geet's mother. Both families sat on the floor during the puja, and the couple did not hold hands. The gifts both families gave one another and their future children-in-law lay carefully folded on the floor. Geet's mother applied sandal paste to Chandana's forehead. When I ask the couple how they felt about having a religious engagement when neither of them actively worship, they explain to me that neither of them objected to making their religious parents happy.

I see a photograph of Chandana's hand. Her engagement ring is like nothing I've ever seen before: in place of where the diamond should be is a single modest pearl. Chandana explains:

> The engagement ring is so fraught with symbolism. As soon as you get engaged you're supposed to stick out your hand and show off your rock. I didn't like that consumerist symbolism. Geet didn't grow up in India so he initially wasn't interested in giving me a diamond ring to symbolize our engagement. Later, however, when he saw how much my mother and his wanted me to wear a ring, he began demanding I wear one. I was perplexed by how much our mothers wanted me to have a diamond engagement ring.

Chandana was surprised by Geet, her mother and future mother-in-law's insistence that she wear a traditional engagement ring, a custom specific to the western world that has only recently gained in popularity among urban middle-to-upper Indians in India. Chandana compromised by requesting a pearl engagement ring. When asked about her decision, Geet tells me that although at first he rejected the idea, over the course of time he's developed more of an understanding of it. Geet strategically refuses to commit his acceptance of Chandana's decision.

Chandana and Geet's engagement distinguishes them from their peers. Chandana's contemplation of the compatibility of householder responsibilities with career aspirations was the only time in my interviews when an Indian-American Hindu woman voiced concern over combining traditional Indian expectations for a wife with modern American ones for a career woman.

Like Nalin and Hamsa, Chandana and Geet combined a private proposal with a public religious engagement ceremony followed by a reception. But whereas Nalin and Hamsa's religious engagement was private, Chandana and Geet's was on a scale closer to that of a typical American wedding (following the ceremony, a hundred and twenty guests attended a buffet lunch reception). Chandana and Geet's engagement ceremony also contained elements similar to that of a traditional Indian wedding: family members were invited to participate in the ritual, and the bride- and groom-to-be both changed their clothes during the ritual. Rather than participate in the customary dowry system, both families exchanged gifts, giving the otherwise traditional ceremony a modern twist. Finally, whereas Nalin and Hamsa were agents in their religious engagement, Chandana and Geet were directed by their family and priest.

The most crucial difference that emerges when comparing Nalin and Hamsa's engagement story with Chandana and Geet's occurs when Chandana initially declined to wear an engagement ring and then subsequently requested a pearl one rather than a traditional diamond ring. Annoyed and confused that her mother and future mother-in-law insisted Chandana wear an engagement ring, a characteristically American symbol, she half declined to express her symbolic ethnic-American identity by wearing a pearl one.

Although Chandana and Geet did not hesitate to participate in a Hindu engagement ritual, Chandana was initially adamant about not participating in the typically American ritual of accepting a diamond engagement ring, thereby symbolically rejecting her identity as an American woman. Immigrant parents, along with most of the second-generation Indian-American men and women I met, took interest in the second generation expressing both their ethnic and American identities. Equally as significant that their son or daughter marry an Indian Hindu who moves fluently between the smaller Indian community and mainstream America is the second generation's participation in both Indian and American rituals as a way to express an ethnic-American identity.

Whereas Hamsa and Nalin's as well as Chandana and Geet's engagement stories are telling of the hold Hindu identity has on second-generation Indian-American Hindus on the brink of marriage, Sapna and Satish's narrative is interesting for its characteristically mainstream American nature and its downplay of Hindu religious custom. Rather than revolving around the couple's bond with one another or their shared Hindu identities, Sapna and Satish's engagement centered on choosing the perfect diamond ring.

It has been three months since I had seen Sapna and Satish at their wedding. I almost don't recognize Sapna. Her hair is now shoulder-length and a pair of glasses sits on her nose. Both she and Satish wear jeans and cotton T-shirts, clothing more casual than when I first met them, at their wedding, when Sapna was dressed in full Indian wedding attire (a sari, gold jewelry and flowers in her hair) and Satish in a white South Indian dhoti (traditional South Indian wedding garb for a groom).

Born in Queens, Sapna moved with her family at the age of seven to Tarrytown where she lived until attending Smith College in Massachusetts before moving to New Jersey to pursue a career in Information Technology. Her parents, originally from Delhi, are active in the Maharashtran community. Both her parents have M.A. degrees: her mother in occupational therapy and her father in architecture (a degree he has employed for not-for-profit projects like renovating Hindu temples).

Satish was born and raised in Delhi where his parents had moved in the 1960s after leaving Madras in South India. He attended an all-boys school in Bombay where he learned Hindi; up until then he spoke English exclusively with his parents and friends. Satish received his M.B.A. in Puna and moved to New Jersey in 2000. He is proud to have lived in cosmopolitan Bombay and describes his parents as modern and progressive; his dad was a Vice President in engineering and his mother received her Ph.D. in Politics with a specialty in the French economy. Satish describes his parents as having a "semi-arranged marriage": both families knew each other and, after meeting for two days, his parents decided to marry.

When I ask Sapna to describe her community growing up, she tells me that her father's Indian architect friends made up a large social network. Upon moving to Tarrytown where Sapna went to high school, her own Indian-American social network grew. In describing her relationships with her parents' Indian friends' children and her own Indian-American friends, however, she tells me that "there was nothing Indian about my relationships. We played the way normal kids did."

Sapna describes how she attended the Ganesha temple on a monthly basis. However, she does not consider herself religious. Religion, she explains, is a "part of my identity with my family it has familial rather than religious significance." Satish argues that Hinduism is not a religion, but a way of life, a description that came up often while conducting my interviews. According to the second-generation Indian-American Hindus I met, because Hinduism does not have an equivalent of the Bible or Quran and because Hindus do not missionize, Hinduism is less a religion and more a philosophy.

Like the other Indian-American Hindus I interviewed, Sapna was not allowed to date in high school, but she did date behind her parents' backs in college. Upon graduating, she explains, her parents encouraged her to date with the intent of marriage, much like other participants in my study whose parents' sole focus was that their children find a spouse. Satish's family's attitude towards their son dating was similar to the restrictive philosophy of Sapna's parents'. In India, Satish says, "everybody focuses on studies." However, after he settled in Princeton, his parents, still in India, put pressure on him to marry and suggested they could introduce him to eligible young women in India via a network of family and friends.

Sapna and Satish met at work where they were both consultants. Two months later, Satish's parents visited the United States and, although it was in the early stages of their relationship, Sapna met them. Satish tells me, "I told my parents about Sapna very early on. It was better to tell them something is going on over here and avoid the problem of arranged marriage. I knew they were looking in India." A year later, Sapna introduced Satish to her parents. After initially rejecting the notion of her American daughter getting seriously involved with and marrying a man from India who might have traditional expectations in a wife, Sapna's parents came around. Once they accepted the seriousness of their relationship, her parents (like Nalin and Hamsa's) pressured the two to get engaged. Sapna tells me, "They said that if we were dating, we might as well get engaged."

Next, Sapna embarked on the quest for the perfect diamond engagement ring. Satish tells me that he thinks "the ring was a bigger deal to her than the marriage itself!" They laugh. Satish continues, "I didn't know how big the ring thing was until I came to the United States." Sapna then describes how she bought a girlfriend of hers to the jewelry store to pick up the ring. Sapna's girlfriend was in awe. Turning to Sapna, she teased: "Sparkle, sparkle, it is very nice!" Sapna agreed and left the store with the ring in her purse and a smile on her face. Sapna, Satish, and their friend went out to dinner where the friend pointed out that "the difference between Sapna's diamond engagement ring and the ones on the street is that hers sparkles despite the restaurant's dim lighting."

When I ask Satish why he went ring shopping with Sapna, he says, "She wouldn't be surprised by the proposal, so why not bring her ring shopping as well?" Sapna adds that she "didn't care about the traditional Indian wedding jewelry because I knew I'd never wear it again." Her diamond ring was a different story.

With the ring set aside for a few months, Sapna's mother made an appointment to check out a potential reception hall one Saturday. The appointment prompted the couple to get engaged. Sapna describes how she and Satish stood in her parents' kitchen while her mother did puja on the kitchen floor. Both sets of parents had parties in their respective homes so their friends could meet their child's future spouse, but apart from the quick prayer there was no real ceremony.

These three couples' engagements suggest three different trends in the engagement proposal ritual among Indian-American Hindus. First, the engagements typically contain the defining characteristic of *both* traditional Indian *and* modern American engagement customs. Almost always, they combine a religious Hindu element such as puja with the romantic American tradition of spontaneously proposing with a diamond engagement ring. The solution, in short, is both/and, rather than either/or. Second-generation Indian-American Hindus are not expected to choose between the American love marriage model or the premodern Indian arranged marriage model. Instead, a third model has emerged, the arranged meeting. Likewise, upon getting engaged, second-generation Indian-American Hindus are expected to participate in both the American diamond engagement ritual as well as a traditional Hindu puja. The engagement is a moment where a couple expresses both their American identity and ethnic background.

Nalin, Geet and Satish's proposals vary slightly, but they all confirm that, along with the wedding day festivities, the proposal is a key moment where Indian-American Hindus express both their Hinduness and their Americanness. Being Hindu, in other words, is their way of being American. All of the second-generation Indian-American Hindus I met are what I call "occasional Hindus," Hindus who were more religious on some occasions, the engagement rite-of-passage in particular. Hamsa and Nalin's decision to pray together, and Chandana and Satish's pujas with their families demonstrate how second-generation Hindus who lead predominantly secular lives participate in religious rituals during key rites-of-passage.

Whereas contemporary, mainstream American engagements are for the most part void of religious prayer, I found that attending temple or doing puja are customary in engagement culture among second-generation Indian-American Hindus. Along with prayer, however, second-generation Indian-American Hindus also embrace the American custom of proposing with a diamond ring. Typically, second-generation Indian-American Hindu proposals and weddings are overwhelmingly religious in tone, expressing ties to India, as well as conspicuous in nature, conveying symbolic ethnic American capital.

Second, I argue that the religious as well as dramatic nature of the engagement proposal in the second-generation Indian-American Hindu population foreshadows the decadent American reception that will follow the overwhelmingly religious Hindu matrimonials on the wedding day. Thus, the wedding day's tendency to combine conspicuous consumption with a display of Indian culture actually begins with the engagement proposal.

A lavish engagement proposal foreshadows the opulent wedding in my discussion of the religious nature of Hindu Indian Americans' marriage proposals. The religious nature of engagements among second-generation Indian-American Hindus foreshadows the overwhelming display of ethnic objects and adherence to religious tradition on the wedding day through the use of Indian ethnic clothing, marrying under a mandap (the religious structure under which Hindus marry), exclusively serving Indian food and playing Indian music, as well as conducting Hindu religious customs such as the sapta-padi (essential seven-step fire ceremony in the Hindu wedding ritual). The conspicuously consumptive nature of engagements among Indian-American Hindus when they participate in the mainstream American diamond engagement ritual expresses ties to mainstream American culture and is meant to reflect the lavishness of the couple's wedding as well as suggest the nature of the couple's marriage: one which conveys affluence.

Finally, I posit that second-generation Indian-American Hindus walk a fine line when attempting to express their American identity and their Indian-Hindu background. The couples I interviewed identified strongly with their American upbringing when they participated in activities such as covertly dating before marriage, proposing with a diamond engagement ring, or getting married without their families' involvement, all typically mainstream American practices incompatible with orthodox Indian Hindu tradition. In order to regain a more balanced ethnic-American identity, the three couples I described followed their private, secular American proposal with a religious ritual.

The Engagement as a Public Religious Event

The public nature of marriage proposals among Indian-American Hindus is a consequence of this generation's desire to articulate their Hinduness and publicly claim their ties to India. Whereas the typical mainstream American engagement ritual is a private one between two individuals, my interviews suggested that engagements among second-generation Indian-American Hindus are more often than not public events that involve both sets of parents as well as siblings. Almost half the couples I interviewed had one or both sets of parents conduct a puja, or host a religious engagement ceremony in tandem with the private proposal. Deciding to get engaged or proposing without consulting the immigrant generation is seen as detracting from the engagement's significance. The second generation found it crucial to have their engagement blessed by their parents and extended family.

Having a private engagement is costly for my participants who have spent their entire adult lives demonstrating their interest in Indian culture by belonging to ethnic organizations and participating in religious rituals. Since family participation is considered a necessary element in having a proper engagement among immigrant Indian-American Hindus, when second-generation Indian-American Hindus have private engagements, they minimize their adherence to Indian tradition in exchange for having a private American engagement. By having a religious engagement ceremony following a private one that involves proposing with a diamond engagement ring, second-generation Indian-American Hindus maintain a balanced ethnic-American identity. A private engagement that involves proposing with a diamond ring is considered as significant as a public religious Hindu engagement by both the immigrant and second generations.

Additionally, I posit that the once-in-a-lifetime nature of proposing marriage combined with the publicity of the event (Chandana's engagement ritual involved extended family members and was followed by a reception for a hundred and twenty guests) makes it a rite-of-passage convenient and practical for second-generation Indian-American Hindus to their connection with India. I describe the women and men I interviewed for my study as "occasional Hindus," people who participated in Hindu religious rituals during key rites-of-passage but for whom daily religious ritual is absent from their lives. Rather than pray on a daily basis at home or regularly attend temple, the second generation expresses Hinduness at symbolic moments in their life. Prayer is not integrated into daily life. The religious engagement's public nature is visible to family and friends and foreshadows the religious tone of the wedding ceremony.

Having a public engagement also cures tensions between second-generation Americans who covertly date behind their parents' backs with the immigrant parents who suffer from religious and social pressures to marry off their children. A public and religious engagement that involves parental participation is the perfect way for the second generation to cleanse themselves of guilt from secretly dating and having premarital sex. By having a public religious engagement, second-generation Indian-American Hindus demonstrate their connection to Indian culture. It also serves as a way for the first generation to feel as if they fulfilled their duty as good Hindu parents by overseeing their child's marriage.

Almost universally, members of the first generation were held responsible for conducting puja while the second generation dutifully followed religious instruction. Chandana and Geet as well as Sapna and Satish were not agents in their religious engagement, and Sapna's obsession with choosing the perfect diamond engagement ring foreshadows the third generation losing some degree of Hindu religious custom when experiencing rites-of-passage.

The Engagement Ring

I argue that the second generation's embrace of proposing marriage with a diamond engagement ring ultimately conveys the same sentiment as having a religious proposal: they both express Americanness. While the religious proposal expresses an Indian-Hindu identity that defines second-generation Indian-American Hindus as ethnic Americans and differentiates them from mainstream Americans, proposing spontaneously with a diamond engagement ring conveys their American identity. Additionally, the religious expression of Hinduness during an en-

gagement puja and the lavishness of the diamond ring that accompanies a sponta-
neous and dramatic proposal both foreshadow the opulent reception that follows
the religious wedding ceremony at second-generation Indian-American Hindus'
weddings.

Chandana's radical feminist disposition separated her from her Hindu peers as
well as from the American mainstream. I propose that the reason why Geet, Chandana's mother and future mother-in-law were so adamant that Chandana wear an
engagement ring was because of the symbolic rejection of her Americanness declining to wear a ring conveyed. As an American woman she is expected to wear
an engagement ring in true American tradition. Declining to wear an engagement
ring suggests an indigence that totally contradicts the traditionally lavish nature
of a typically mainstream American engagement. Ironically, by initially refusing
to wear an engagement ring, Chandana was rejecting her identity as an American
rather than her Indianness. As an American born-and-raised woman, her mother
and future mother-in-law expected Chandana to proudly wear a diamond engagement ring which she half-compensated for by accepting a pearl one.

Spontaneous and Romantic Engagements

Although all my participants recounted engagement stories that included the American tradition of proposing with a ring, romantic engagements are still not popular
among the second-generation Indian-American Hindus I interviewed. However,
five couples out of the twenty I met had proposal stories well-suited for an article in *Modern Bride* magazine. Having only dated a few months, Chitra and her
boyfriend Shiv went ring shopping before Shiv proposed a few minutes after midnight on Valentine's Day. Chitra recounted: "I kept saying how cheesy it would be
if he proposed on Valentine's Day, so he waited until after midnight." Shiv created
a cutout inside a fairytale anthology where he embedded the diamond ring. The
book opened to "The Princess and the Pea" because Shiv's pet name for Chitra is
"Princess." When she opened the children's book and found the ring, he explained
that the book had yet another function: for Chitra to read fairytales to his children.
Chitra describes how the proposal was expected but that:

> It was such a shock in such a form. He still thinks it is the most ingenious
> thing he's ever done in his life. He's very pleased with himself. He had
> to ask me twice because I was in such shock.

Chitra's dramatic engagement story testifies to the power romantic engagement proposals have in American culture. The couple met under unromantic cir-
cumstances (a mutual friend of both families acted as matchmaker to exchange
photographs, phone numbers and particulars such as age, education, and profession). However, Shiv was enticed by the idea of staging a dramatic marriage
proposal where the romantic gesture of presenting Chitra with a book of fairytales
guaranteed his proposal a place as a modern day fairytale. Theirs was a courtship
that espoused their Indianness via their traditionally Indian way of meeting within

their families' networks. What better way is there to "spend" the symbolic ethnic Indian capital they accrued and express their Americanness than on a diamond engagement ring and a Valentine's Day proposal?

Conclusion

Engagements among Indian-American Hindus contain the defining characteristic of both traditional Indian and modern American engagement traditions: engagements almost universally combine a religious Hindu element such as puja with American romance and conspicuous consumption that characterize proposing spontaneously with a diamond engagement ring. After years of participating in Hindu rituals during the holidays, learning an Indian dialect, and belonging to ethnic social organizations, second-generation Indian-American Hindus spend their capital when they participate in mainstream American traditions such as proposing spontaneously with a diamond engagement ring or privately without their parents' involvement. However, having a priest-officiated puja witnessed by both sets of parents enables the young couple to express their Indian-Hindu background.

All of the second-generation Indian-American Hindus I met are what I describe as "occasional Hindus." The engagement proposal is a rite of passage where the second generation displays their ethnic Hindu identity in a symbolic way, often publicly. Rather than integrate worship into their daily life, second-generation Americans articulate their Hinduness symbolically, largely during key rites-of-passage: in this case through prayer and by involving family in the marriage decision-making process.

The first decision after getting engaged is setting the wedding date, but the first decision of major significance for the bride is what she will wear on her wedding day. The bride's costume, whether it is a traditional red silk sari, couture white designer wedding gown, a simple store-bought dress or an outrageous Bollywood-inspired lengha (modern, semi-formal skirt and shirt outfit popular among young Indian women), sets the tone and character of the wedding in addition to communicating to the guests the bride's identity. I examined various bridal styles among second-generation Indian-American Hindu brides I met and interpreted them as one would a novel; the brides' choices are telling, and each dress has its own story.

— 3 —

Wearing Ethnicity: The Indian-American Hindu Bridal Industry

Every second-generation Indian-American Hindu woman knows that, upon get-ting engaged, she must travel to India "for shopping." Newly engaged women and their over-zealous mothers imagine stores and stockrooms full of luxurious silk saris that go on for yards, sparkling with flashing zardozi work and bordered with hand-stitched gold and silver patterns. Convinced that India offers wedding apparel and supplies unrivaled in America, middle-to-upper class Indian fami-lies spend thousands of dollars traveling to India to do their wedding shopping. However, some have to make do in the United States. Hamsa explains somewhat wistfully why she did her shopping in Jackson Heights, Queens:

> I decided not to go to India for shopping. Most of my friends go to India when they get engaged. I felt like I needed to save all my vacation for the wedding. That was a difficult decision because we had to buy a lot of stuff here. We had family buy saris in India for us.

In India, Hamsa's grandmother selected Hamsa's two wedding ceremony saris. Hamsa tells me, "I wore a pink sari and then changed into the traditional red-and-white sari." (Halfway through the Hindu wedding ceremony, the South Indian bride changes into a traditional red-and-white sari to symbolize her status as a newly married woman. Hindu brides rarely wear all-white since white is the color of mourning and worn at funerals).

Although Hamsa relied on her grandmother to purchase wedding ceremony attire, Hamsa chose her own reception outfit, though not without considerate ner-vousness. She said that she was told it was difficult to find a reception outfit in New Jersey. She continues, "However, the first store I went into I found my outfit. I was thrilled with it." Hamsa's story echoes the widespread romance described by mainstream American brides who miraculously "fell in love" with the first gown they tried on. Kismet and fate cropped up in many of the stories I heard about finding the "perfect" wedding outfit.

The wedding photos that hang on Hamsa's wall show her drowning in seem-ingly infinite folds of red silk and burdened by twenty-two karat gold jewelry. Only her hands and head are visible, and the sari's elaborately hand-sewn silver pattern glitters. Her red reception sari masks every nuance of Hamsa's shape. All that is revealed is her radiant and smiling face. Hamsa proudly tells me, "It was expensive. It cost two thousand dollars."

One reason second-generation Indian-American Hindu brides such as Hamsa express regret at not having the opportunity to shop in India for "authentically" Indian bridal clothing is that they are eager to display their Indianness. One way to express their Indian cultural background is by employing material objects such as bridal attire purchased in India and wedding favors and invitations that combine to create a more authentic Indian-Hindu wedding. "Wearing Ethnicity" examines four distinctly different bridal costumes: Hamsa's traditional red-and-white ceremony sari and her red-and-gold reception sari; Sachi's white Vera Wang wedding gown; Ajala's gold lengha; and Savita's red, off-the-rack dress from Macy's. Each outfit represents a different approach to negotiating Americanness and Indianness. For the women who chose to wear distinctly Indian wedding garb such as Hamsa and Ajala, rather than argue that they are rejecting their Americanness, I instead suggest they are displaying their ethnic-American identity.

All four women, despite their disparate choices in bridal "gowns," ultimately express their Americanness by asserting their hyphenated-American ethnic identity. Black Americans, feminists and Native American Indians who have participated in identity politics in the last five decades precede the women I met in my study who predominantly wore Indian bridal clothing in order to publicly and proudly claim their hyphenated-American identity as Indian-American Hindu women.

However, the decision to wear traditional versus modern Indian clothing, couture versus a department store-bought dress is not solely informed by identity politics. The women I met were also negotiating two disparate dreams, one propagated by India's Bollywood movie industry and the other delivered by Hollywood and popular television shows. Choosing a wedding gown is about choosing a dream. Participants negotiated two dreams, one that is Indian and the other American. Whereas Savita decided to find a middle ground and visually embrace both her Americanness and Indianness by wearing a red dress from Macy's, Sachi rejected her Indianness by wearing a white couture gown. Hamsa embraced India of forty years ago in her decision to wear a traditional white-and-red South Indian sari, and Ajala found inspiration in Bollywood when she decided to wear a gold lengha (Figure 3).

Hamsa's Indian-Hindu bridal attire distinguishes her from her mainstream American peers; by wearing it, she claims her identity as an Indian-American. (Hamsa's decision to wear traditional Indian-Hindu bridal clothing reinforces her Indian cultural background while simultaneously expressing her hyphenated ethnic American identity.) However, by displaying her Indianness, Hamsa was also expressing her Americanness, since embracing a religious identity is at the core of expressing a uniquely American one.

When asked if she ever fantasized about wearing a white wedding gown, Hamsa responds:

> I never found the white wedding attractive. From the beginning I knew
> that wasn't my culture. That's not the way I grew up. I didn't say it was

bad or good, I just thought that was the way it was. I knew I would have an Indian wedding. That's the way I grew up, that's the way I was raised. Wearing Indian clothes was what I wanted. I didn't want to wear a suit or plain regular clothes. I wanted to do it the right way. In my mind that was the right way.

Like Hamsa, seventeen out of twenty women said that a white wedding made no sense for them. Almost all explained that having a white wedding seemed inappropriate and not even an option; wearing a white wedding gown was for their white friends, and wearing a red sari is a Hindu woman's birthright.

When I asked Nalin, Hamsa's husband, if he had ever envisioned himself marrying a bride wearing a fitted, strapless ivory gown with a long train rather than the traditional red-and-white sari Hamsa donned on their wedding day, he responded:

I think white gowns are nice but I never thought this needs to be done. I thought [wearing a sari] is more beautiful. We grow up seeing the gown, but now I think wearing a sari was unique and different and so much better.

Nalin, like Hamsa, places traditional Indian clothing on a pedestal; both bride and groom exoticize customary Indian Hindu bridal attire.

Like Hamsa's decision to wear a different outfit for her reception, I found it customary for second-generation Indian-American Hindu brides to relinquish control over what they will wear to their own wedding ceremonies and instead make unilateral decisions about what they will wear to their reception. Typically, a close female relative or future mother-in-law took it upon herself to select the bride's wedding ceremony attire. Whereas traditionally, Indian-Hindu brides have little if any say in what they will wear on their wedding day, mainstream American brides make shopping for their wedding gown the most significant decision in their wedding planning. How do second-generation Indian-American Hindu brides negotiate the mainstream American tradition of a bride searching for the "perfect dress" with the traditional Indian one where the bride has no say in what her family or future mother-in-law chooses for her to wear on her wedding day?

I found that the first- and second-generation Indian-American Hindus have already reached a compromise whereby the bride is expected to wear clothing chosen by her family or future mother-in-law for the ceremony. The bride then changes into an Indian costume of her choice for the American-style wedding reception. This compromise ensures the survival of an ancient Indian Hindu tradition where families choose the bride's wedding attire, ensuring that the bride dresses modestly, even as it offers the bride the opportunity for self-expression at her reception.

When it came to planning the religious wedding ceremony, Hamsa left it to her parents and future in-laws. However, regarding aesthetic choices, Hamsa wanted to make her own decisions. Hamsa tells me it was hard giving up control when her future mother-in-law selected a wedding invitation without Hamsa's input. Hamsa had specific notions about the hall, flowers, invitations and reception outfit she wanted. Like ninety percent of the brides I met in my study, Hamsa wanted Indian objects at her wedding to create an Indian-Hindu aesthetic. She participated eagerly in a burgeoning Southeast Asian Hindu bridal industry that allows future brides to purchase objects that carry symbolic meaning to produce a more authentically Indian Hindu wedding.

Whereas Hamsa and Nalin were eager to wear traditional Indian wedding clothes at their Hindu ceremony, Sachi and Tom opted for a less traditional civil ceremony. Sachi describes her parents:

> My parents were really, really strict. They're both very religious people. My dad is much more conservative than my mom. With my dad, being a father was about being strict, old school, and he focused on how I was his eldest child and only daughter. If I had been a son, maybe, he would have softened up.

Sachi describes talking to other second-generation Indian-American Hindus about their Indian immigrant parents "to get a read on what was going on. When my parents would do or say something I couldn't figure out I assumed it was because they were Indian. We would all compare notes." Sachi equated her parents' strictness with their Indianness. Sachi's decision to wear a white couture Vera Wang wedding gown symbolizes her emotional and intellectual distance from her Indian parents.

Sachi, a Ph.D. candidate in Sociology at University of Pennsylvania where she is studying the South Asian diaspora, married Tom, an atheist lawyer educated at University of Pennsylvania's Law School. They are one of four ethnically mixed couples I interviewed in my study and the only one to have two ceremonies (Hindu and civil) on their wedding day. I gathered from our time together that much of Sachi's interest in having a civil ceremony was because she:

> Wanted a bridal shower with my friends, and a bridal party where my friends would be included, and to go shopping for a white wedding gown and go for fittings.

Sachi aspired to have all the pre-wedding and wedding day activities her friends and other young women fantasize about in mainstream America. And, of the twenty women I met in my study, Sachi was the sole one to wear a white wedding gown.

Sachi's lifelong conflict with her parents led her to equate their idiosyncrasies and rigidity with their Indian-Hindu identity. Rather than eagerly claim her ethnic culture and Hindu religious identity she instead demonstrated no interest in displaying her Indian background. Some might say that her lack of interest in staging a traditional Hindu wedding is rooted in the fact that she married a non-Hindu Indian, a white atheist. I posit instead that her tense relationship with her parents motivated her to incorporate the aesthetics of a white wedding rather than a traditional Hindu one into her wedding day festivities.

What does this mean about Sachi's Indianness or Americanness? I read Sachi's lack of interest in wearing a sari as a way to distance herself from her parents and reject her Indianness. Amazed to hear that none of the second-generation Indian-American Hindu brides I met in my interviews ever fantasized about wearing a white wedding gown, I was relieved to meet Sachi who openly described the high-end, distinctly American objects at her wedding (Crane's invitations, a couture Vera Wang wedding gown, Kate's Paperie wedding programs). Rather than sound like her second-generation Indian-American Hindu peers, Sachi more closely resembled the white, mainstream American readers of *Modern Bride* or *Elegant Bride* magazines. Sachi was more interested in having a conspicuous wedding that would display her family's affluence and her high-end taste rather than an ethnic wedding that would display both her ethnic identity and her family's financial success. Sachi's decision to have an American civil ceremony and to continue wearing her white wedding gown to her reception illustrates not only her claim to Americanness but also her emotional and intellectual distance from her parents.

Over bagels and orange juice, Sachi tells me that her father is from a small village in Andrapradhesh, South India. He completed his M.A. and Ph.D. in Mechanical Engineering in the United States. In the interim, he visited India in 1969 where a marriage broker in his village arranged for Sachi's father to meet Sachi's mother. She tells me, "There was a space of seven days between knowing both families existed and my parents' wedding." At the time, Sachi's mother was an Economics lecturer.

Sachi's parents were founding members of a temple in New Jersey. Her parents' religious devotion often conflicted with Sachi's happiness when she was a teenager. When I ask her if her parents allowed her to date in high school, she responds with a simple "No." She recalls how after fighting for weeks, her parents finally relented and allowed her to attend her senior prom with girl friends. She describes prom dress shopping with her mother:

> I was so exhausted [from fighting] that I just couldn't get into it. My mother was completely prepared to pay for my prom dress, for something I picked out, but I ended up borrowing something from a friend.

She met Tom when they were both sophomores at New York University. After two years of dating seriously, Sachi introduced Tom to her parents as simply a "friend." Tom chitchatted with her father for only a few minutes, but later her father told her not to bring Tom to the house again. She describes her reaction: "I was grateful to my dad for how he worded it. I hated being deceptive and feeling the need to be deceptive. Even if I had to be deceptive from now on I rationalized that I was following the letter of the law." When I asked Tom how he felt about being kept a secret, he explains:

At first I pushed her to address the tensions between her and her parents. I very much wanted her to tell them what she was doing and that she was an adult. I was annoyed by her unwillingness. She was annoyed with me. In retrospect she was right to handle it the way she did. She was not trying to use me as a weapon of independence from her parents. If she was she could have been more blunt and forward about it, but it wouldn't have been to say, "I really like this guy."

Immediately following graduation, Sachi told her parents that she was still seeing Tom. She describes her mother as hysterically crying and her father as angry. But, she continues, "I'm sure there are certain things they said that they have tried to forget themselves. My relationship with my parents is very different now from what it was before I got married." When I ask her if they reacted that emotionally because they wanted to arrange her marriage, she describes the almost complete absence of discussion regarding Sachi ever marrying:

> My parents never talked to me about marriage. My dad firmly believed in marriage, but it was always in the abstract, never practically speaking in direct application to me. He believed in firm parental involvement. I remember him helping a friend try to find a groom for the friend's daughter. He came home with a stack of bio-datas, resumes that had photographs attached, and he defended his belief in the custom of arranging marriages.

Once he found out she had been secretly dating Tom for four years, Sachi's father asked her "not to make me a grandfather" before she was married. Sachi interprets her father's statement as a concern on her parents' part that they could not express:

> They were worried that having a boyfriend for me meant something different than having a girlfriend meant to Tom because he was white or "American" as they put it. They thought I was taking the relationship more seriously. I was just trying to have a boyfriend but my parents were asking me if he was going to marry me. It was hard to explain to my parents that we didn't talk or think about getting engaged.

Sachi describes a culture gap between herself and her parents. Since dating, what Americans see as the stage before marriage, was nonexistent in their lives, Sachi's parents had no frame of reference for what dating meant.

Sachi tells me, "Then I moved to Hong with Tom. That was the next disaster." When she told her parents she was moving with Tom to Hong Kong where he would work for a hedge fund, Sachi's father threatened not to talk to her again, and her mother asked dramatic questions like, "What's going to happen to you?!"

Six months after moving back to the United States from Hong Kong, Tom proposed to Sachi during intermission at a New York Philharmonic concert at

Carnegie Hall. Two elderly ladies seated behind them clapped and smiled, asking to view the ring, and the couple coolly continued to watch the remainder of the performance. Sachi tells me with a little laugh, "I think it was my dad's real hope that Tom would marry me because he was concerned that, if Tom wouldn't, who would?" Sachi was further annoyed when her mother refused to tell family and close friends about the engagement and forbade Sachi from wearing her diamond engagement ring to parties and temple functions.

For her civil ceremony and reception, Sachi wore a loosely fitted white Vera Wang wedding gown she found in a vintage bridal store on the Upper East Side, but she wore a sari chosen by a close family friend, or "auntie," for the Hindu ceremony. She tells me, "The sari wound up being really nice. It wasn't a full onslaught of red." Although dismissive of her parents' Indian values and culture and after living with Tom in Hong Kong and dating against her parents' wishes, Sachi agreed to display her ethnic-Indian background at her Hindu wedding ceremony by agreeing to wear a sari. However, she was determined to continue expressing her Americanness and distance herself from her parents by wearing a couture white wedding gown for her civil ceremony and reception.

Sachi happily describes how she found her couture wedding gown, but she admits she was disappointed when her mother refused to accompany Sachi to the various bridal salons. Like her peers, Sachi fantasized about shopping with her mother for the dress Sachi would wear on the most important day of her life. Rolling her eyes, she recounts her mother's advice "not to spend too much money and to try to buy something I could wear again."

Sachi's description of her wedding gown shopping experience more closely resembles that of mainstream American brides of Judeo-Christian background rather than Indian-American Hindu ones:

> I bought a Vera Wang dress for less than a thousand dollars at a vintage store. I was excited because the dresses I saw at RK Bridal weren't as nice and were more expensive. I was glad that my dress was silk and organza, not synthetic. The dress moves where you move. I was glad that it was simple. The problem became how was I going to fit into the dress?

Sachi was in love with the idea of wearing a designer gown rather than one from a store that resembled a warehouse, RK Bridal, and relished the gown's simplicity, its quality and ability to show her feminine form.

In addition to declining to wear Indian clothes for much of her wedding day, Sachi's rejection of her Indianness also played a role in a dispute with her father over the wedding invitation. Her father wanted a traditional red one with the image of Ganesh gracing its cover. Sachi, however, wanted a western one. She explains: "I am very into paper, and I wanted a Crane's invitation. I'll just say it. I took control over the invitations, bless my dad. I even made the programs." Sachi purchased blank white paper from Kate's Paperie and designed her wedding program with purple ribbon and Asian stamps in honor of their time living together in Asia. Sachi chose to express sophisticated American taste by purchasing distinctly American wedding objects such as Crane's wedding invitations.

Even Sachi's mother failed to understand the importance of having beautiful western objects at her daughter's wedding. Sachi and her mother's conflicting views towards the significance of finding the perfect wedding gown and having a beautiful bridal bouquet demonstrates the disparate philosophies behind what is central in an Indian-Hindu wedding as opposed to an American one. Even wedding planning with Sachi's normally uncommunicative mother created conflict. Sachi describes her argument with her mother over the bridal bouquet:

> I wanted stephanotis [a white flower popular among American brides] in my bridal bouquet. That added twenty dollars to the cost of my bouquet so my mom told the florist to forgo the stephanotis. I couldn't say anything, but the florist politely intervened and kindly said that there were other ways of cutting costs and that "we should let the bride have her bouquet." The incident shows my mom's zaniness; why should twenty dollars be an issue in this hugely expensive wedding?

Whereas Sachi and the florist subscribed to the notion that the bride is central in the wedding, Sachi's mother saw her daughter wearing a beautiful and expensive gown while carrying a bountiful bridal bouquet as insignificant. Both philosophies highlight the contradistinct ways in which Indian Hindu and mainstream American weddings are structured and organized in addition to commenting on Indian Hindu versus mainstream American attitudes towards a bride's display of her sexuality on her wedding day.

Sachi is an anomaly because she never expressed excitement or eagerness for displaying her ethnic-Indian identity even though she wore a sari to her Hindu ceremony. Despite her parents' roles as founders of a Hindu temple and keepers of a devout household, Sachi had little interest in displaying her Indianness at a point in her life when her peers were flying to India and attending bridal expos locally to haggle for the most ethnic wedding objects they could muster. I interpreted her lack of interest in displaying her Indianness as a response to lifelong tensions she had with her parents. Sachi, rather than display her Indian identity, instead expressed her Americanness at her wedding.

Wearing Ethnicity

Although Sachi was the single bride out of twenty I interviewed to wear a traditional western bridal gown, all twenty agreed that the bride's outfit is the single most significant symbol at a wedding. Only three out of twenty second-generation Indian-American Hindu women I met refrained from wearing a traditional sari at their wedding. The vast majority of the women I interviewed defended the aesthetics of a traditional Hindu wedding and deemed Indian wedding saris more beautiful than what they saw as plain, run-of-the-mill white wedding gowns. These women pointed to the richness of a red sari, the brilliance of gold wedding jewelry, and the intricacy of henna (drawn patterns) on a married woman's hands to show me what beauty bedazzled them.

However, I believe that more insidious reasons motivate the expectation that second-generation Indian-American Hindu women wear traditional wedding attire on their wedding day, as Sachi's mother's reluctance to shop with her daughter for a wedding gown intimates. I came across disparate views on what the bride should symbolize with her wedding garments. Whereas in mainstream American weddings, brides popularly wear strapless, fitted gowns to convey their womanhood and femininity, the traditional Indian Hindu bride is expected to act demurely and dress modestly, neither spotlighting her feminine form nor positioning herself as central to the day's festivities. Marriage for an Indian-Hindu bride symbolizes embracing a new set of responsibilities that include passing on tradition and acting as a conduit for culture. Women, in any culture, are traditionally seen as the conduit for culture, religion, and family values. Therefore, for a second-generation Indian-American bride, wearing western wedding clothes suggests a threat to Old World tradition. Wearing red and behaving modestly expresses a more traditional Indian mindset, whereas placing oneself at the center of attention rejects Indians' expectations that brides act demurely.

Time and time again, the women I interviewed described to me their eagerness to wear traditional Hindu wedding garb as a way to confirm their identity as Indian Hindus to their family and friends. Whereas some may perceive these women's enthusiasm for wearing traditional wedding clothes as a rejection of modernity, I would argue that the second-generation Indian-American Hindu women I met who were adamant about wearing traditional Indian-Hindu bridal attire were, in fact, demonstrating their modernity. In fact, by wearing ethnic clothing at their wedding they were establishing themselves as ethnic hyphenated Americans. The reason why seventeen out of the twenty women I interviewed recoiled at the idea of wearing a white wedding gown was not because they deemed it as American, but because wearing traditional Indian wedding garb was, paradoxically, more American.

By claiming their Indian-Hindu identity, the women embraced their minority status as Indian-American Hindus and transformed an otherwise neutral identity on the American landscape to one that is positively scripted. By wearing a sari, a second-generation Indian-American Hindu could articulate her Indian background as well as distinguish herself from the mainstream. Wearing a white gown would ignore her ancestry, family network, ethnic and religious community, as well as diminish her ethnic Americanness.

In addition to drawing from pre-modern India from which the tradition of wearing a red wedding sari originated, India's movie industry, Bollywood, is a crucial cultural force for second-generation Indian-American Hindu women eager to articulate their ethnic-American identity. Bollywood India is a third culture to emerge as operating in the lives of second-generation Indian-American men and women planning their weddings. Mira Nair's film *The Namesake* (2006) playfully points out the second generation's obsession with Bollywood in a scene where the main characters, Gogol Ganguli and his wife Moushumi Mazumdar (played by Kal Penn and Zuleikha Robinson) perform a Bollywood-inspired dance on their wedding night. While all the wedding photographs I examined in my interviews contained some element of Bollywood in the Indian photographer's posing of the bride and groom, Ajala, whose story I describe later in the chapter, in particular took the popularity of Bollywood among Indian-American Hindus to a whole new level.

A significant reason why second-generation Indian-American brides have not been seduced by mainstream American tradition is because India's Bollywood consistently provides blockbuster films that exhibit Indian-Hindu wedding customs. Mainstream American women in the United States look to Hollywood movies such as *My Best Friend's Wedding* (1997), *The Wedding Date* (2005), *Monster-in-Law* (2005), and *Sex and the City* (2008) for inspiration regarding their own wedding day (which flowers to use, what invitations to buy, what gown style is most in vogue right now). However, even Hindu wedding customs are infiltrating the mainstream. In the independent movie *Rachel Getting Married* (2008), the white heroine and her bridesmaids wear saris while the African-American groom dons a traditional kurta and garland.

Similarly to Hollywood, Southeast Asian women have Bollywood hits to offer guidance for their own wedding planning. More recently, movies starring Southeast Asians marketed towards western audiences (for example, Mira Nair's *Monsoon Wedding* (2001) and Gurinder Chadha's *Bride and Prejudice* (2004)) expose second-generation Indian-American Hindus to South Asian wedding aesthetics. In fact, Anjala described to me how her white Methodist boyfriend's family had seen *Monsoon Wedding* and were excited to attend a big Indian wedding. Due to a short wedding planning timeline, Ajala was forced to have a small civil ceremony, disappointing her future in-laws. In Bollywood films, the focus tends to be on the conspicuously consumptive rather than religious aspects of the wedding celebration-the mendhi party and baraat rather than walking around the fire or kanyadan. Planning an Indian-Hindu wedding is not only a way to display one's Indian-Hindu cultural background but is also an expression of one's affluence.

Constructing India through Conspicuous Consumption

Most of the men and women I met belong to a specific socio-economic class: most are daughters and sons of medical doctors, accountants, engineers, architects and professors, and many have themselves earned graduate degrees in such fields as medicine, engineering, law, education and business. I ascribe their desire to wear ethnic wedding clothes as a result of when status anxieties were lower, success in America has led obstacles like racism to recede. Marilyn Halter in *Shopping for Identity* writes,

> Ethnic identification persists and the research demonstrates that higher socioeconomic status and increased educational levels have strengthened rather than weakened it. Explicit ethnic identification has become an indicator of economic success and integration. What used to be a liability

has now become an asset, a luxury of assimilation. [1]

Inspiring "shock and awe" among guests towards the bride's display of her ethnic identity requires money. At the heart of the event is shopping and there are many ways to purchase one's dress, invitations, place cards or flowers whether it is through the Internet, from a local vendor, or via mail-order catalogue. By participating in conspicuous consumption (renting a twenty-five hundred dollar mandap, buying plane tickets to India, purchasing fifteen hundred dollars worth of wedding invitations and a two-thousand dollar silk wedding sari, renting a horse for the baraat from the local stable for a thousand dollars, and hiring a table duo for fifteen hundred), couples engaged in consumerism in order to emphasize their identity as second-generation Indian-American Hindus.

I discovered a booming South Asian American Hindu bridal industry in America for second-generation Indian-American Hindu brides unable to travel to India for their wedding shopping. Instead, these women attended bridal expos such as the Dulhan Expo (Figure 4a/4b) where they could purchase distinctly ethnic bridal fashion, decorations and wedding services. Rather than read *Modern Bride* and *Elegant Bride*, my participants subscribed to *Shaadi Stlye* and *Bibi Magazine*. Instead of surfing weddingchannel.com or theknot.com, the women I met were on WeddingSutra.com and benzerworld.com.

Whereas India has made strides towards modernity, the immigrant generation describes an India from forty years ago to their second-generation American children, bequeathing antiquated notions of what it is to be Indian. Hamsa's red-and-white South Indian wedding sari and her gold-and-red reception outfit are informed by Indian wedding traditions from forty years ago when the first generation immigrated to the United States. The vast majority of women I interviewed were intent on displaying their Indianness. This expression included dressing modestly and acting demurely on their wedding day. Strictly adhering to traditional Indian-Hindu notions of bridal modesty is another way for a second-generation Indian-American Hindu woman to convey her ethnic Americanness. Rather than reject her family's impulse to drape her in yards of silk, the typical bride willingly accepts her role and is conscious that her appearance is critical in inducing an aura of collective nostalgia for India at her wedding.

The wedding day is a significant moment where second-generation Indian-American Hindus convey their ethnic American heritage and religious identity in ways that don't interfere with their modern lifestyles. "Occasional Hindus" have daily lives that more closely resemble those of their mainstream American peers than those of their parents. Second-generation Indian-American Hindus wear American clothes, eat American food, work in diverse professional settings, date and co-habit before getting married, drink alcohol, have premarital sex, and rarely worship. Yet when it comes to the wedding day no expenses are spared to keep them from exhibiting the rich cultural origin that distinguishes the second generation from the somewhat ordinary co-worker or next door neighbor with the same credentials and lifestyle but who lack an exotic eastern background.

Conspicuous consumption plays a critical role in planning an authentic Indian-Hindu wedding. There is no getting around the fact that having an ethnic and traditional wedding requires means. Therefore, the second-generation Indian-American Hindu weddings I examined are not only meant to express ethnic-American identity but are also a forum for conveying affluence and immigrant success. No doubt, having an Indian-American Hindu wedding includes all the impulses towards lavishness described in mainstream American weddings. Here, I describe a bridal industry that targets second-generation Indian-American Hindu women eager to display their ethnic-American identity and the immigrant generation's material success.

Just as second-generation Indian-American Hindus can use the Internet as a source in providing eligible marital candidates, the Web has become a significant tool in collecting the ethnic objects necessary to orchestrate an authentic Indian-Hindu wedding. Archana ordered her reception outfit on-line from a website popular among Indian women who live in the United States and England. Women with means are known to purchase their wedding clothes from the popular Benzer website. On benzerworld.com, a woman can choose from a range of Indian wedding clothes: a sky blue gangra, choli, and dupatta in silk tissue, all embellished with heavy antique silver zardozi and diamente embroider for a cool $2,169; or a rust-colored pure georgette paneled ghangra choli and dupatta all embellished in resham, stone and zardozi work for a mere $2,679.

Even mainstream American wedding websites such as modernbride.com offer insight on how to plan an Indian-Hindu wedding. The "Real Brides" link offers advice from married Hindu women, and the "Multicultural" link displays stories from couples whose weddings are labeled by the website as "Indian-Hindi & American," "Indian-Hindi & Catholic," "Indian-Hindi & Christian," and "Indian & Nondenominational" for brides who are planning "inter-ethnic or bi-religious weddings." Stories are submitted by couples such as "Ashni and Chris in New York" or "Rupam and Mickey in Los Angeles" and contain color photographs of their exotic Indian wedding. *Modern Bride* targets women with high-end tastes and big wedding budgets so it is no surprise that publishing photographs from Indian weddings is popular among the staff at modernbride.com. The American bridal industry is aware of the Indian community's willingness to spend large amounts of cash on a wedding. Displaying Indian weddings on their website is a way to pander to an elite population with money to spend in addition to conveying mainstream America's interest in eastern traditions.

Magazines such as *Bibi* and *Shaadi Style* (Figure 5), along with websites such as WeddingSutra, focus on planning Indian-Hindu weddings. *Bibi*, whose headquarters are in Texas, is a fashion magazine for Indian-American women, but wedding vendors take up most of the magazine's advertisement space. Companies such as Elegant Affairs (Figure 6a/6b) and Saida's Decorations rent out mandaps in addition to offering "onsite specialty preparation of multi cultural cuisine (puris, kabobs and breads)" and "sangeet, mendhi, & garba decorations."

Shaadi Style magazine is based out of Boston and contains advertisements that are clearly focused on having a distinctly Indian-Hindu wedding; mandap decorators advertise their services as do Indian clothing designers such as Ritu Kumar who is based in India but has established herself as a formidable force in the Indian fashion industry worldwide. White gowns are absent from the magazines pages, which eschew popular western models such as Kate Moss or Cindy Crawford for Bollywood actress Aishwarya Rai. The twelve month wedding checklist published in every issue of *Modern Bride* has its counterpart in *Shaadi Style*, but along with reminding the bride to set a wedding date, it also suggests picking dates for the garba, sangeet and the mendhi. In addition to offering suggestions for registering, *Shaadi Style* publishes articles such as "Building Your Trousseau," a custom popular among Indian-American-Hindu brides who are expected to wear gold jewelry throughout their pre-wedding and wedding day festivities.

Magazines such as *Shaadi Style* and websites like benzerworld.com make having an authentic Indian-Hindu wedding possible for American women like Hamsa and Archana who live in the United States. Websites such as Wedding-Sutra.com has functions offered by mainstream websites like theknot.com including building a personal wedding webpage, creating a guest manager, and keeping a wedding checklist. The site contains articles on wedding day beauty such as hints on how to inexpensively bleach skin and have long lasting mendhi. Finally, WeddingSutra.com contains hundreds of images of eastern bridal attire, making finding a wedding ceremony sari and reception lengha all possible at the click of a mouse. And, of course, a credit card with a generous limit helps. The Southeast Asian American bridal industry attests that although money can't buy love, it can buy ethnicity.

Bollywood Bride

Jingle jingle. Before even seeing Ajala walk down the aisle, the guests hear her walking towards Mitch, her White Methodist groom. It is her wedding day and she is wearing a self-described "Vegas gold" lengha (modern and fitted long skirt and short-sleeve or sleeveless Indian costume for young women; the equivalent of a black cocktail dress) she had custom-made in India. Ajala's wedding lengha attests to the influence Bollywood fashion has on bridal clothing worn by second-generation Indian-American Hindus in the United States. Two Indias emerged in wedding culture among middle-to-upper-class second-generation Indian-American Hindus: India from forty years ago and contemporary Bollywood. The two Indias exhibit themselves side by side at Indian-American Hindu weddings and eloquently express confusion on the part of the second generation. The disparate resources second-generation Indian-American Hindus draw on for their cultural knowledge and religious identity come from their parents and imported Bollywood films.

The lengha is heavily decorated with gold and silver bells. Tiny mirrors embellish the outfit, reflecting sunlight in different directions. Ajala's headpiece is an orange-gold twenty-two karat necklace woven into the middle parting in her hair that ends with a pendant that rests on her forehead. A string of small tikkas sit above her eyebrows and a large red one smack in between. Around her neck and wrists are pieces of twenty-two karat gold characteristic of the wedding jewelry offered in the little jewelry boutiques found on 74th Street in Jackson Heights, Queens. Putting on no pretense of acting as a demure Hindu bride, Ajala glows in her purposefully Bollywood wedding apparel that is meant to distinguish her from her female guests clad in traditional saris.

Unable to find a Hindu priest willing to conduct a Hindu wedding ceremony for Ajala and her Methodist boyfriend, the couple opted to have an outdoor civil ceremony. The civil ceremony had elements more in common with a white, mainstream American wedding such as a procession, vows read out loud by the couple, a recitation of a poem, and a kiss to seal the marriage. However, despite choosing to have a civil ceremony rather than a Hindu one, it was important to Ajala that she wear something Indian:

> I didn't like the colors and styles available in western wedding dresses. One way to display my identity and provide solidarity with the married Indian women in my family since I wasn't doing the rituals was by wearing something Indian. I did do mendhi. I did it as a little girl at my cousin's wedding and loved it. Those were the two non-negotiable things for my wedding planning.

Ajala also wore her grandmother's ring and bangle as a way to feel a connection to her ancestors. However, the road toward deciding on her wedding garb was a difficult one that involved many misadventures and obstacles.

Ajala, upset that she could not have the Hindu wedding ceremony she'd always imagined for herself, felt it important that she wear Indian clothing as a way to convey her connection to India and her Hindu upbringing as well as display her Indian heritage. Like seventeen of the twenty women I interviewed, Ajala was uncomfortable with the idea of wearing a white wedding gown. She tried her best to create an Indian aesthetic for her appearance on her wedding day by wearing tikkas (colorful dots) on her forehead, twenty-two karat gold characteristic of Indian brides, and mendhi on her hands and feet. Cultural continuity was important to Ajala, and wearing Indian clothes, despite its Bollywood film flavor, along with her grandmother's jewelry, was her way of expressing her Indian-Hindu identity and differentiate herself from her white American peers.

The "Vegas gold" lengha she wore to her wedding and the Indian food she served at her reception were two ways Ajala displayed her Indianness. Ethnic clothes and foods are the two most popular and easily attainable objects for second-generation Indian-American brides and their mothers. Eager to convey her Indian heritage and horrified at the thought of guests interpreting her civil ceremony as a rejection of her ethnic-American identity, Ajala was intent on purchasing as many ethnic objects as she could afford to orchestrate an Indian wedding.

Although wearing a red sari would have been the easiest way for Ajala to express her Indianness as well as display her ethnic-Americanness, an "American" thought persisted in nagging her. Upset that members of her boyfriend's family were wearing saris to her wedding, Ajala felt the need to differentiate herself from her new white sisters-in-law and assert her Indianness. Just as Sachi's mother declined to accompany her daughter in gown shopping, Ajala's mother thought it uncouth for Ajala to spend so much time ruminating on what she would wear for her wedding. Generational conflict over what a second-generation bride should wear is a theme in the interviews I conducted. Issues of different views towards a woman's sexuality surfaced when members of the immigrant generation argued what the bride wore didn't matter.

Ajala's decision to model her bridal apparel after a lengha worn by Madhuri Dixit in a blockbuster Bollywood film suggests the infiltration of Bollywood culture in the weddings of second-generation Indian-American Hindu women. Much like the mermaid shape was made popular among mainstream American brides after Monica Geller played by Courteney Cox wore a plunging V-neck gown with a mermaid silhouette in her wedding to Chandler Bing in the American hit show *Friends*, second-generation Indian-American brides make fashion decisions on their wedding day that are influenced by the modern day Bollywood India films. Websites such as WeddingSutra.com exhibit photographs of what famous Hollywood as well as Bollywood stars wore on their wedding day. Second-generation Indian-American Hindu brides view not only Cindy Crawford in her John Galliano slip-dress but also Twinkle Khanna in her Abu Jani-Sandeep Khosla red sari.

Finally, Ajala's delight at wearing a lengha made in India and designed by fashion designer Archana Kochar positions her as participating in consuming cultural artifacts and products that help build one's ethnicity identity. Ajala saw purchasing an Indian lengha from Jackson Heights as a step below having an outfit made in India. The bridal outfit was more authentic for Ajala because of its Indian origin and served as a valuable prop in distinguishing herself from her future sisters-in-laws who wore Indian saris to the wedding.

Whereas the traditional Hindu wedding bridal outfit is a red sari, Ajala wore a "Vegas gold" lengha. Having always imagined herself wearing a red sari at her wedding, Ajala was stumped when her mother bought a maroon sari for one of Ajala's future sister-in-laws. Ajala explains how Mitch's sisters and mother all wanted to wear saris at the wedding and how Ajala's mother bought them each a silk one from India as gifts. Initially shocked by their interest in wearing saris, Ajala later decided it was that decision that made her wedding unique. "It was a beautiful gesture, but I guess it was the American bride in me who wanted to be the center of attention." Stunned that her mother had bought a maroon sari that so closely resembled Ajala's red one, she refused to wear it on the grounds that it would make her blend in and look like a guest at her own wedding.

Although all but two of the twenty brides I met drew from Bollywood in planning their wedding receptions, only Ajala let Bollywood inspire her decision on what to wear to her ceremony. After traditional India, from which the immigrant generation came of age, and mainstream American culture as typified by popular culture, Bollywood India was a third culture to emerge in how second-generation Indian-American Hindus plan their wedding. Bollywood is the already-established "mediating culture" between traditional India and modern America. It is the default middle position where love marriages exist within an Indian framework.

Ajala's dress is a unified and material display that conveys both her Indian heritage and her American identity. After months of rummaging through the clothing boutiques in Jackson Heights and unable to find clothes to suit her modern and American taste, Ajala had her lengha made in India, something she thought "was kind of cool." "I loved my dress," she explained. "I was looking at the pictures recently. My dress looks great in pictures. I wanted something Indian from India." She felt that having her lengha made in India lent an authenticity to her wedding dress even though her guests were unaware of its origin.

A Hindu-Western Compromise

One woman I met in my study struggled with finding a way to convey both her heritage and her American upbringing in a financially savvy way that would accommodate her planning a wedding over a short engagement period with limited resources. Savita, a law school student at Emory, and her boyfriend Dev, a Ph.D. candidate at University of Virginia, did not have the time or the money to shop in India during their six-month engagement. Rather than wear an off-the-rack white American wedding gown (since white signifies mourning among Hindus), or black (because the color suggests mourning among Americans), she chose to wear a modest, red floor-length, spaghetti-strapped western dress from Macy's. At her wedding, she tells me, "A lot of people were confused by that."

Having witnessed Dev's family plan his brother's large Hindu wedding the previous year, neither Dev nor Savita wanted a big Indian wedding. Dev's mother wanted a Hindu ceremony for her son and was unhappy when the couple decided to have a civil ceremony instead. When I asked Savita why she didn't want a traditional Indian wedding and how her friends and family responded to it, she tells me:

> We didn't want halogen lamps, cloth napkins, and fifty percent of the guests people we didn't know. I didn't want the insanity going into a large wedding for logistical decisions. I decided to have my own wedding and do a religious ceremony later. Also, I wanted to change [the Hindu ceremony] up a bit and have it be less sexist. As for friends and family, we don't know people that would have judged us for having a civil ceremony or would have had high expectations that we have a big religious wedding.

Savita, who is actively involved in community service organizations that aid women who suffer from domestic violence, likens organizing their wedding to a political event:

> We rented a hundred and fifteen chairs and had it at a friend's house. We created a chart of everyone's responsibilities such as picking up the cake, etc. Everyone wanted to do a job. Everybody pitched it. It was a community event. Our moms cooked. We had the chicken tikka masala

and paneer catered. My mom made Mexican eggplant and French macaroni. We had puti and samosas after the ceremony. We made our own invitation; it had a mendhi pattern on it. Even a friend of ours who is a magistrate officiated the ceremony rather than some crusty old man completely uninterested in us who would run through some lines quickly so he could get to the next wedding.

Savita and Dev's wedding is one of three where the bride and groom were interested in not only displaying their Indian heritage at their ceremony by invoking Hindu spirituality and having friends perform the tabla, but also conveying their symbolic ethnic American values by walking down an aisle and reciting vows. In a clear violation of Indian protocol of the demure bride, Savita took center stage by walking down the aisle unescorted in her red western dress, introducing the readers in her civil ceremony, and reciting her own vows.

Savita and Dev's wedding demonstrates how expressing one's Indian cultural background on one's wedding day often involves displaying ethnic objects which is inextricable from displaying affluence and participating in conspicuous consumption. Two graduate students unable to muster the resources to plan an authentic Indian-Hindu wedding, Savita and Dev drew from friends and family for Indian entertainment, the tabla performance, Indian food, and "Indian" wedding invitations designed with mendhi patterns rather than Ganesha's image. The couple wished to avoid the chaos and conspicuous consumption involved in having a traditional Indian wedding. However, the couple was not entirely uninterested in displaying their ethnic-American identity. By offering Indian and American food and playing Indian music as well as adapting a Judeo-Christian format for their ceremony, the couple articulated their ethnic-American identity despite their small budget.

What Men Want (to Wear)

In my study, men also wore ethnic clothing to express Indianness. I was surprised by the number of second-generation Indian-American Hindu men who wore traditional Indian clothing such as a kurta (matching tunic and baggy pants outfit worn as the equivalent of a tuxedo) (Figure 7) or dhoti (white fabric wrapped around a man's waist usually worn by South Indian Hindu grooms) (Figure 8) to their wedding ceremony. Like their brides, the grooms were expected to wear Indian wedding attire for the ceremony before changing into a tuxedo or suit for the reception. Even Tom, a white atheist, had not put much thought into why he wore a kurta: "I felt that wearing Indian clothes was just part of the ceremony. I thought that wearing American clothes would be very strange." I interpret Tom's explanation as an admission of sorts that a function of Sachi's Hindu wedding ceremony was to convey the family's Indianness to family and friends. Wearing a western tuxedo or suit would have interfered with the symbolism behind the Hindu ceremony.

When asked why he wore a traditional Gujurati wedding outfit, Nalin responded: "In my mind that was the right way." Wearing Indian clothing was vital for conveying his identity as an ethnic American, part and parcel of the larger project of having an authentic Indian-Hindu wedding. Only Samir made a compromise regarding wearing a dhoti to his wedding: "My work colleagues were going to be at my wedding so I thought it would be odd not to wear a shirt at my wedding." Although he wore a loose sheet around his waist, he refused to go shirtless.

Conclusion

The four different bridal outfits illustrate the fact that consumerism is inextricably tied to displaying Indian-American identity. The modern practice of shopping for ethnicity helps ethnic Americans display their cultural and religious identities. The lavishness behind shopping for ethnicity enables ethnic Americans to convey their material success. As is true for mainstream American brides who wish to convey their affluence, second-generation Indian-American Hindu brides choose their bridal attire based on the degree to which they want to express their Indianness and their affluence.

Women like Hamsa had three silk outfits for her wedding festivitiesone pink sari, one red-and-white sari, and a final red lengha for the reception. Wearing the wedding saris given to her by her future mother-in-law at the ceremony enabled Hamsa to satisfy Indian tradition while expressing American values such as agency and individualism by wearing a self-chosen red lengha to her reception. Women such as Savita, who paid for her own wedding, bought a red dress off the rack. She saw her compromise as enabling her to express her ethnic-American identity without requiring she spend two thousand dollars on a traditional wedding sari or couture wedding gown.

Sachi, for whom having a connection with India and Hindusim was fraught with tension due to the strained relationship she had with her parents, chose a white wedding gown as a way to express her American identity, distance herself from her parents and reject her Indianness, ignoring the display of ethnic objects that interested her peers. Finally, Ajala, in her desire to be a unique bride as well as display her ethnic identity, wore a Bollywood-inspired lengha that served to display both her Indian cultural background and her American identity despite not having a Hindu wedding ceremony. Her gold lengha is a literal depiction of how Bollywood has successfully embraced American ideals and values such as joy, love, and romance in an Indian framework.

Although eager to display their Indianness, second-generation Hindu Indian American women who wore traditional red saris (seventeen out of twenty of the women I interviewed) were also intent on choosing their own wedding clothes. The compromise, unspoken but universal, was that whereas family chose the bride's clothes for her ceremony, the bride selected her own reception outfit. This unspoken compromise meets the desires and philosophies of both the first and the second generation. By allowing figures from the first generation to choose the bride's wedding ceremony clothes, the bride is preserving an age-old tradition of parental involvement as well as accumulating and displaying symbolic ethnic Indian capital while allowing the first generation to participate in an age-old tradition of selecting the bride's clothes and ensuring her ability to induce an aura of collective nostalgia for India at the wedding. Assuming the bridal ceremony outfit is as demure as tradition dictates, the bride also allows her family to preserve her reputation as sexually pure.

The first three chapters of *Bollywood Weddings* have focused on the wedding planning that precedes such pre-wedding and wedding day festivities as the mendhi party, bridal shower, and sangeet. I argue that ethnic Americans gain value in the marriage market and otherwise in their community when they display their ties to Indian culture and embrace American tradition. Marrying an individual with symbolic ethnic Indian capital increases one's own, just like wearing ethnic bridal attire articulates claims to an ethnic identity. Finally, I argue that when the immigrant and second generations display Indianness at weddings they are also articulating their affluence. Staging an authentic and traditional Hindu wedding is impossible without conspicuous consumption as my description of the burgeoning Southeast Asian bridal industry attests.

The final two chapters will examine pre-wedding and wedding day festivities among second-generation, upper-to-middle-class Indian-American Hindus. By elucidating which rituals and elements of ritual survive the passage to America, as well as which fall by the wayside, I hope to articulate how second-generation Indian-American Hindus construct Indianness and Americanness.

In Chapters 4 and 5, I extend the meanings of symbolic ethnic Indian and American capital by applying them to the specific religious and social rituals and traditions both mainstream America and traditional Indian-Hindu culture offer to second-generation Indian-American Hindus. By examining the choices second-generation Indian-American Hindus make in planning pre-wedding and wedding day festivities, how they negotiate the demand to their American identity and Indian background, and in the process feel at home as ethnic-Americans, one may come to a better understanding of how the second generation formulates their own identities as well as construe what is and is not American.

Notes

1. Marilyn Halter, *Shopping for Identity: The Marketing of Ethnicity* (New York: Schocken Books, 2000), 10.

— 4 —

Pre-Wedding Rituals: The Both/And Model

"Well, you are going to have a mendhi party, aren't you?" Friends and family often pose questions like this one to newly-engaged, second-generation Indian-American Hindu women. Such questions regarding wedding planning convey the community's expectations concerning a proper Indian-Hindu wedding. A wedding absent pre-wedding traditions such as a mendhi party (when women gather to have their hands and feet decorated with intricate body paint before the wedding) or baraat (a procession of friends and family who lead the groom sitting on a horse to the wedding hall) detract from one's Indianness. However, while the immigrant generation expects the second generation to participate in traditional pre-wedding customs, both generations also embrace mainstream American pre-wedding traditions such as the bridal shower.

Just as the immigrant generation expects their American-born children to accept the arranged meeting model for marriage, which embraces both traditional Indian as well as modern American notions about marriage, having an engagement that includes proposing privately with a diamond ring and participating in a religious ceremony, and wearing traditional Indian bridal attire during the ceremony followed by a more western outfit of the bride's choice for the reception, the first generation expects the second generation to integrate both American and Indian-Hindu pre-wedding day festivities. By examining the customs of four couples prior to their wedding days, this chapter concludes that the immigrant generation embraces both American as well as Indian-Hindu traditions for the purposes of community building.

Additionally, while the immigrant generation is invested in raising children that display their Indianness, the first generation also expects its children to express their American identity because Americanness symbolizes the immigrant generation's success in integrating into mainstream America and adopting American culture. The second generation is likewise eager to participate in both American as well as Indian-Hindu pre-wedding customs because these activities are sanctioned by the first generation and allow couples to express both their Indianness and Americanness. Rites of passage such as having a religious engagement, hosting a baraat, or throwing a mendhi party provide occasional Hindus with opportunities to step out of secular life and assert their Hindu religious identity.

I posit that rather than define themselves as solely Indian Hindu or American, second-generation Indian-American Hindus struggle to maintain a balance whereby they can assert their American upbringing as well as confirm their ethnic identity rather than choose between the two. A central observation in my study is that although pre-wedding and wedding day events among second-generation Indian-American Hindus are characterized by Indian-Hindu images, songs, food, clothes and language, couples also assert their American identity which is sometimes overlooked underneath all the ethnic decor.

Both Hamsa and Nalin's families hosted a variety of pre-wedding rituals while the couple was engaged. Hamsa's parents threw a non-religious barbeque engagement party in their backyard and designated the driveway as a dance floor. In front of seventy of their closest family and friends, Hamsa's father presented Nalin with a suit. Nalin's parents instructed the couple to feed each other cake. Hamsa describes it as "weird I think it is a custom in his family that they feed each other cake at all celebrations." Nalin explains: "At most of the functions I went to growing up, they fed each other cake. And I saw it in American culture as well so I accepted it as a universal cultural thing. We do it at more formal types of functions." Feeding cake is not a tradition exclusive to weddings in Nalin's family. Family members feed each other cake at birthdays, graduations, and engagement parties. In mainstream American weddings, couples feed each other cake for good luck. Perhaps the Kilis were exposed to the tradition of feeding cake after attending an American colleague's wedding. For the Kilis, feeding each other cake, a public and an affectionate gesture, conveys their love for one another.

The Kilis adopted an American tradition that expresses intimacy, so much so that the public display of affection (rare in India) put Hamsa ill at ease. Feeding cake to a family member is an American tradition the Kilis adopted to express their adoption of American values they deem as positive, affection, in a way that also enabled them to convey their close family ties, characteristic of their community-oriented and family-building Indian values. Thus, feeding cake serves to both assert Indianness and Americanness.

Following the backyard barbeque, Nalin's parents hosted a hundred and fifty guests at their home in Ohio. Nalin's family organized their son's engagement party by appealing to traditional Indian-Hindu culture and tradition when they asked a half dozen Swaminarayan priests to conduct a puja in their home. As is customary, the women were separated from the men since Swaminarayan priests cannot be within women's viewing range. The women sat in the Kilis' living room as they strained their necks to catch a glimpse of the engagement ceremony in an adjoining room. Nalin and his father sat in American suits beside the family's home shrine, a place in the home where images in the form of statues of Hindu gods are organized for private worship. The Swaminarayan priests were fully hidden in saffron-colored robes that covered their bodies from head to toe. They wore orange hoods over their heads so that only their faces were visible as they chanted and prayed aloud for guests to follow in unison. The women entered the shrine room upon the priests' exit and covered Nalin's hands and face with tumeric, a yellow paste popularly used in Indian cooking. They also placed a bright orange garland around his neck, concluding the religious engagement party. The puja served to celebrate Nalin's rite of passage from single life to the brink of marriage.

Participating in the puja was a way for Nalin, an "occasional Hindu," to participate in a religious ritual at a significant moment in his life after having an otherwise mainstream American-style courtship. Additionally, despite living a largely secular life that more closely resembles that of his fraternity brothers than that of his parents, the engagement ceremony allowed Nalin to assert his identity as an Indian-American.

Hamsa's family hosted an engagement party that resembled a typical mainstream American one rather than the religious ceremony Nalin's family arranged, but both were invaluable for an ethnic-American identity. The first engagement party was a mixed-gender celebration and a forum where the couple could publicly display affection as they fed each other cake. However, feeding each other cake served a double function: to confirm their western-style courtship as well as to convey their family-values, what they deem as a characteristic of their Indian heritage. Finally, Nalin's family held a religious ceremony that allowed Nalin to express his religious Indian background.

Engagement parties are significant for second-generation Indian-American Hindu couples and their families because these parties typically serve as the first time when the bride and groom's extended families and family friends meet. After years of covert dating and months of negotiating the marriage proposal, the engagement party serves as a public blessing on behalf of the couple's families. In addition to revealing their son's and daughter's choice of a spouse, the engagement party symbolizes the first generation's endorsement of the marital union. The engagement party legitimizes the American-style courtship and is a way for the couple to display ties to their Indian culture after years of unsanctioned dating which, in most cases, included premarital sex. Additionally, hosting an engagement party is a way for immigrant parents to feel as if they have fulfilled their responsibility as parents by ensuring their child marry. Whether or not the parents were involved in setting up their child's marriage, hosting an engagement party symbolizes their participation and involvement in marrying off their child, bringing the parents closer to vanaprasthya where they spend less time on responsibilities associated with family life and more time in worship.

Although there is no equivalent to bachelor or bachelorette parties in Hindu India, both Hamsa and Nalin participated in the sort of debauchery expected in a typical American stag party. Hamsa gleefully recalls: "We started at three in the afternoon and drank a lot of tequila at Tortilla Flats before going to a Chippendales show. It was really hilarious. We went to my friend's house afterwards and played all these games." Nalin arranged for twenty high school and college buddies to meet him in Orlando, Florida, where they played golf, went white water rafting and attended strip clubs. Nalin explains, "It was more symbolic, going to the strip club. The bachelor party is more for the others to have fun than for the groom." Both Hamsa and Nalin participated in classically American pre-wedding events that confirmed their identities as Americans who lead secular lives. However, Nalin, in contrast to Otnes and Pleck, suggests the significance of the bachelor party is for his community's benefit. Nalin describes his bachelor party as serving a double function. Asserting his identity as an American bachelor soon to be married while confirming his investment in his community, a traditionally Indian value. Pre-wedding events such as engagement and bachelor parties were described across-the-board by the participants in my study as events staged for family and friends eager to participate in the impending marital union, conveying that the focus of the event was not on the couple but on community-building.

In an example of the more culturally mixed and religiously ambiguous traditions I observed, Hamsa's mother threw her daughter a bridal shower, a mainstream American pre-wedding custom that has no equivalent among Hindus in India. Whereas bridal showers, in which friends give gifts such as household appliances to a newly engaged woman, do not have a parallel in India (often Indian families present the couple with a check or cash, but gift-giving is not considered necessary), women of the immigrant generation have embraced this mainstream American tradition. Rather than see the event as a way for second-generation women to "upgrade" their home by collecting updated and more expensive versions of household items they already own, second-generation Indian-American women use the bridal shower as a way to gather friends and family of her and her mother's generation together.

Hamsa's elderly "aunties" (her mother's friends) entertained themselves by playing Scrabble while Hamsa's girlfriends chatted with one another and nibbled on samosas. Wearing a traditional, sky-blue Punjabi salwar-kumee (a popular matching tunic and baggy pants outfit intended for everyday use), Hamsa sat in the designated "bridal chair" and was forced to wear wrapping paper and ribbon on her head as she opened gifts. Anchored above the chair, hanging over Hamsa's head, was a white "bridal shower umbrella."

When asked about the umbrella, she is mystified. "I guess it's a bridal shower umbrella one of my aunts made for the occasion," she explains hesitantly. Hamsa's aunties took it upon themselves to create an elaborate decorative space for the bride-to-be to reside under while opening her gifts. White lace hung from the white umbrella's periphery, mimicking the traditional mandap in the Hindu wedding ceremony. The mandap designates the space in which the couple weds and the priest presides. It is a holy wedding space and comprises of a raised platform with a canopy. Unbeknownst to her, Hamsa's aunties created a sacred canopy under which Hamsa could receive her gifts, adding a religious flavor to her culturally ethnic bridal shower. Hamsa's aunties not only created a makeshift mandap but also provided shelter for her as she was rained upon with gifts.

The first generation embraces mainstream American traditions like the bridal shower for two reasons. The first reason is the desire for more pre-wedding events to build community. The second is to display the first generation's successful integration into American society. Second-generation Indian Americans often host pre-wedding festivities that are hybrid in nature, such as Hamsa's bridal shower where she un-wrapped gifts under a bridal shower umbrella which doubled as a mandap. The bridal shower confirmed Hamsa's identity as an American woman on the brink of marriage while demonstrating her Indian family values by inviting women from her mother's generation who created a sacred space for Hamsa as she participated in mainstream American pre-wedding practices.

Perhaps the most significant and widespread pre-wedding ritual among Indian Hindu women is the mendhi party. Here a professional mendhi artist is hired to draw elaborate designs on the hands of the bride, her mother, friends, aunties, and young female cousins. Mendhi is a type of body make-up exclusive to Hindu weddings. The vast majority of the women I met described to me the significance of having mendhi done in their wedding. Getting mendhi done is as widespread and popular a symbol as wearing a red sari on a Hindu bride's wedding day.

Hamsa thought her mendhi party was more for her younger sister and her friends' benefit: "We had four women doing mendhi and for many of the girls it was their first time getting it done." "Getting mendhi done" is a tradition that has survived immigration and is very popular among second-generation Indian-American Hindu women. Mendhi parties serve as a conditioning force for young Indian-American Hindu women. Just like serving as a flower girl indoctrinates a young woman into Judeo-Christian wedding culture, young cousins and sisters often begin their education in Indian-Hindu wedding culture at their first mendhi party. Female participants echoed each other when they described to me how ever since they attended their first mendhi party as a little girl they always knew they would want to "get mendhi done" for their wedding day. Mendhi is the ultimate sign of a woman's marital status on her wedding day and in the weeks prior to the event. The sight of mendhi on a young bride's hands is a particularly visible display of symbolic ethnic Indian capital, making mendhi parties a popular pre-wedding custom among both the immigrant and second generations alike.

Like Hamsa, Ajala was adamant that she have mendhi done on her hands. She explains: "One way to display my identity and provide solidarity with the married Indian women in my family since I wasn't doing the rituals was by wearing something Indian. I did do mendhi. I did it as a little girl at my cousin's wedding and loved it. Those were the two non-negotiable things for my wedding planning." As a young girl, Ajala was in awe of mendhi's intricate patterns and fantasized about getting mendhi done when it was her time to marry.

Whereas books such as Cele C. Otnes and Elizabeth H. Pleck's *Cinderella Dreams: The Allure of the Lavish Wedding* (2003) focus on the role of conspicuous consumption in mainstream American pre-wedding events, I emphasize the familial, religious and communitarian elements of traditions among the weddings I observed. Ties to Indian heritage and culture, Hinduism, and family values motivate the first generation to accept and embrace American pre-wedding traditions. Rather than detract from their ethnic background, engaging in American traditions such as having a bridal shower works to build connections between the couple's family and friends. Additionally, participating in both mainstream American and Indian-Hindu pre-wedding traditions provides opportunities for second-generation Indian-American Hindus both to express their Indian-American identity.

Just like Bollywood inspired Ajala in choosing her bridal outfit, India's movie industry also factored into how couples planned pre-wedding events. Kirti, a Johns Hopkins University-educated news broacaster, and her husband Naresh, a Philadelphia-based photographer, planned their pre-wedding functions and wedding day around a Bollywood theme. Their pre-wedding events convey the cultural impact Bollywood has on Indian-American Hindu wedding culture among the second generation. Kirti and Naresh, unlike Hamsa and Nalin, chose the Bollywood dream rather than draw from traditional Indian and American traditions that inspired Hamsa and Nalin in their pre-wedding events. Although Kirti and Naresh did not have mainstream American pre-wedding events like the bachelor and bachelorette parties or bridal shower, they did have a mendhi party and sangeet.

Kirti and Naresh's Bollywood theme expresses the romantic, whirlwind courtship that preceded it. Kirti tells me in the car on the way to the local court in Edison, New Jersey, where Kirti and Naresh will legally marry to as to keep Naresh from getting deported to India: "Oh, yes, we knew very quickly after we met that this was it." Theirs was a precariously American whirlwind courtship which included a six-month-long, hot-and-heavy courtship which resulted in an unplanned pregnancy. The Bollywood-themed wedding allowed the couple to express ties to India while staying true to their romantic and impulsive personalities. Whereas many of the brides and grooms I met appealed to both the staid, traditional India of the 1960s that their parents left upon immigrating to the States as well as the romantic India presented in the film industry, Kirti and Naresh solely drew their inspiration for their wedding extravaganza from Bollywood.

The couple's shot-gun wedding followed a courtship full of impulse, passion, and American-style romance. Advertisements in *India Abroad*, family networking, and posting a profile on shaadi.com are absent from Naresh and Kirti's story of how they met. However, Naresh and Kirti, rather than hide their atypical Indian-Hindu courtship instead adapted it as a story fit for a modern Bollywood romance. Bollywood India is the third culture to emerge as a mediating culture between premodern India and mainstream America. Bollywood India is where western values such as love, romance, and impulse fit in mainstream Indian culture. Kirti's wedding website describes how after the two met at a mutual friend's birthday party, the couple commenced a courtship that "spanned several continents, hundreds of e-mails, thousands of miles by plane, train and automobile." A photograph of Naresh and Kirti, heads bowed towards one another so their foreheads touch, is displayed on the website's home page. Behind them is a photo-edited field of flowers and blue sky.

Something about the photograph nags me. I've seen the image before and I'm not sure where. I quickly realize that I've seen something like this image, not once before but hundreds of times. The composition of the couples' bowed heads and the pastoral background, the blue clouds and pink petals, recall memories of poster advertisements for countless Bollywood films. Aptly, their wedding website is titled, "A Love Story Made for Bollywood."

Rather than quietly marry in a small ceremony attended by a few close family members and friends in order to avoid having to hide Kirti's ballooning middle-section, Kirti and Naresh staged a wedding weekend, a tradition made popular, according to Otnes and Pleck, by affluent Americans. Eager to celebrate their shared Indian heritage, the couple staged a whirlwind series of traditionally Indian-Hindu pre-wedding events which included a Thursday night mendhi party, Friday night sangeet, and Saturday wedding and reception. By hosting Indian pre-wedding activities inspired by Bollywood, the couple was able to express their Indianness despite what their community deemed as the couple's unconventional vocations

Figure 1.   Kavita and her mom on the author's wedding day. Kavita wore a custom-made gown made of two silk saris while her mother wore a traditional sari.

Figure 2.   A mandap is the religious structure in which Hindus marry.

Figure 3. Ajala wore a "Vegas" gold lengha at her wedding.

Figure 4a. A postcard advertisement for the Dulhan Expo, a wedding planning expo which targets second-generation, South Asian women who live in the New York tri-state area.

Figure 4b. A postcard advertisement for the Dulhan Expo, a wedding planning expo which targets second-generation, South Asian women who live in the New York tri-state area.

The Premier South Asian Wedding and Fashion Magazine

Fall / Winter 2004

SHAADI
Style

Trendy
Mehndi

5 FABULOUS
HONEYMOON
HOTSPOTS

Celebrating
Gujarati Style

Menu
Planning 101

Trousseau Tips
a guide to post honeymoon style

137
GLOBAL
INSPIRATIONS

*Cake
Couture*

Plus:
Unique Rings
Centerpieces
Bridal Showers
Photojournalism

USA $5.00 Canada $7.50
4 3>

0 7447058266 3

Figure 5.   *Shadi Style,* a bridal magazine for second-generation Indian-American women.

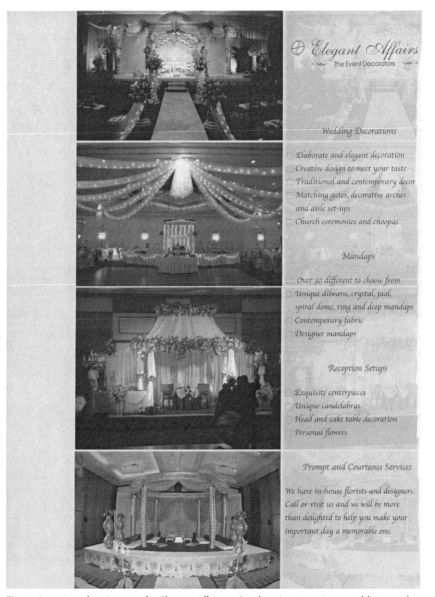

Figure 6a.   An advertisement for Elegant Affairs, a South-Asian American wedding vendor.

Figure 6b.   An advertisement for Elegant Affairs, a South-Asian American wedding vendor.

Figure 7. A groom wears a kurta at his Hundu wedding ceremony.

Figure 8.   Satish wore a dhoti in his South-Indian wedding ceremony.

Figure 9. Nalin rode a horse at his baraat.

Figure 10. Kirti had an ice sculpture chiseled in Ganesha's form at her Bollywood-themed wedding reception.

and their passionate romance.

Fifty close family members and friends gathered on Thursday evening for the mendhi party in one of the convention rooms at the hotel where the couple would hold their wedding two days later. Children as young as eight to "aunties" as advanced in age as Kirti's grandmothers swarmed the room. The chatter among the women, the Bollywood music in the background, and the echo of the room made hearing anything clearly nearly impossible. Anju, the mendhi artist, quickly and quietly arranged her work station and busily started applying mendhi. Whereas the older women refrained from having mendhi applied, the younger ones were delighted by the intricate designs on their skin. However, when instructed that they couldn't touch anything, the young girls voiced sighs of regret at having to sit patiently while the mendhi dried. Kirti, clad in a voluminous pink sari meant to hide her pregnancy, talked to her aunties and young guests alike. All the women and children wore colorful Indian clothes, a stark contrast to the sterile nature of the hotel convention room. Two of Kirti's friends distributed goodie bags containing a DVD of the couple's favorite Bollywood hits.

Kirti and Naresh held their sangeet, a night of singing and dancing for the couple's close friends and contemporaries, at Akbar, a popular Indian restaurant in Garden City, Long Island. Naresh orchestrated the night's festivities and hired a deejay to play hybrid bhangra-American music. A four-tiered, raspberry-filled cake with ivory icing sat tall on a table for all the young guests to view. Sangeet night is a popular pre-wedding tradition in India in the weeks leading up to the wedding. It is an event where musically gifted friends and family sing bajaans (religious songs that celebrate the love of God) and contemporary Bollywood songs as well as perform choreographed dances for guests. This elaborate event very closely resembles a wedding reception because guests expect a cake, catered food, and a professional deejay.

Whereas sangeets are in India, this tradition is less common among Indian-American Hindus. Unlike the mendhi party which sixteen of the twenty women I interviewed hosted in the weeks leading up to their wedding, only Naresh and Kirti had a sangeet. One reason why the sangeet is not as popular in America as it is in India is because it makes the wedding reception redundant. Whereas in India, friends and family pitch in by making rotis and curries for days before the event and a friend volunteers to play music, hosting a sangeet in America is as expensive as holding a second wedding reception. Additionally, a sangeet threatens and undermines the importance of the wedding reception itself, something couples are loath to do.

The absence of forums to learn to sing and dance is another reason why the sangeet has fallen by the wayside among second-generation Indian-American Hindus. A sangeet requires family and friends to comfortably dance and sing in front of guests. Indian-America's small size and dispersal around the United States offer few opportunities to hone one's ability to play the sitar or dance like a Bollywood movie star. Finally, the demise of the sangeet itself makes for fewer opportunities to acquire the talents needed to keep the sangeet up and running.

Since second-generation Indian-American Hindus typically host both traditionally American and Indian-Hindu pre-wedding festivities, it is even more imperative that the couple register for gifts. However, even where a bride registers says something about her identity. Chandana describes her most difficult decision in wedding planning was deciding where to register. In her "futile attempt to be iconoclastic," Chandana decided to choose a set of charities for guests to donate rather than register at stores like Tiffany's, Saks Fifth Avenue, and Crate & Barrel. Chandana's mother knew that few guests from the first generation would feel comfortable giving to charity, pointing out that "the desis will give junk from their closets" before giving to UNICEF (desis is a slang word to describe Southeast Asian Indians.) Chandana's decision to ask guests to donate to charity fails to express either strong ties to America *or* India. By refraining from having a traditional registry, Chandana failed to identify herself as espousing American values even as she diminished her identification with Indian ones.

Chandana and her mother compromised after Geet, Chandana's husband, suggested they give their guests a choice. Guests could have the option of purchasing a traditional gift from a department store if they did not feel comfortable giving to charity. Chandana registered at Macy's rather than Bergdorf Goodman or Bloomingdale's, popular stores among people in Chandana's community. Chandana also registered at JustGive.org where she selected ASHA, a well-known organization that promotes primary education for poor women and girls in India, and a second charity for South Asian women who have experienced domestic violence. Registering at Macy's conveyed Chandana's symbolic ethnic American and Indian capital. Asking guests to donate to charity made her identity more ambiguous.

Conclusion

The multitude of pre-wedding events Indian-American Hindus participate in such as the mendhi, sangeet, or religious engagement parties serve as forums whereby family and friends have the opportunity to strengthen their social bonds within a small community. Indian Hindus of both the immigrant and second generations embrace non-religious as well as religious pre-wedding functions and deem them as invaluable for Americanness as well as Indianness. The non-religious engagement party allows the couple to convey the American-style courtship preceding their engagement whereas the religious engagement party enables the couple to assert their Indianness after having an American-style courtship. Pre-wedding Indian-Hindu traditions such as the mendhi party and sangeet allow second-generation Indian-Americans to participate in Indian-Hindu customs during key rites of passage, highlighting their status as occasional Hindus.

Although the sangeet has fallen away as an insignificant pre-wedding ritual among second-generation Indian-American Hindus, the mendhi party functions as a significant socializing factor in indoctrinating second-generation Indian-American Hindu women to Indian-Hindu bridal culture. Mendhi continues to have a distinct symbolic association with marriage.

The concluding chapter of *Bollywood Weddings* focuses on the various elements that make up the Hindu wedding-day ritual and the significance of these elements among second-generation Indian-American Hindus. By examining the traditional as well as evolved meanings of the stages that make up the Hindu wedding ceremony, we can observe how certain traditions survive or fall away, much like how the mendhi party thrives among second-generation Indian-American Hindu women whereas the sangeet has all but perished. By examining which elements of the traditional Hindu wedding ceremony perpetuate and which are extinguished, we can better understand what conditions need to exist for tradition to continue.

—5—

The Wedding Day: Improvising on Hindu and American Traditions

One of the central findings in my research is that two diametrically opposed Indias coexist in wedding culture among second-generation Indian-American Hindus: traditional Indian culture from the 1960s when the first generation immigrated to the States and contemporary Bollywood culture where romance and extravagant weddings are the central scenes around which drama ensues. The baraat, a North Indian Gujarati tradition where the groom arrives at the wedding site on a white horse followed by clapping and dancing guests, appeals to both conservative India and Bollywood as well as the third source of wedding culture, mainstream America. The groom's baraat on the wedding day is equivalent to the bride's mendhi party prior to the wedding. Both are seen as necessary elements for having an authentic Indian wedding. Half of the grooms I met had a baraat prior to the wedding ceremony.

At Nalin's baraat, guests danced to the beat of a drummer; friends and family did ras garba (a group dance where participants clap hands and take steps in unison) alongside Nalin who was mounted on a white horse. A mystified local stable owner led Nalin's horse through the parking lot to the entrance of the hotel where Nalin would marry Hamsa later that day.

The white horse was dressed in Hindu wedding colors, orange, red and gold finery, but simultaneously appealed to the age-old western symbol of the knight in shining armor galloping on a splendid horse to rescue his future bride (Figure 9). The baraat appeals to both Americans and Indians because the groom makes a grand entrance that is compatible with both cultures' stories and traditions. Additionally, Nalin's arrival on a white horse parallels the mainstream American groom arriving at the church in a white limousine. Subsequently, Nalin's Gujarati baraat enabled him to identify with Indian-Hindu and American wedding customs. Although Nalin did not wear shining armor, he looked princely in his white kurta and shell-shaped ivory headpiece. When asked why he wore a traditional Gujarati wedding outfit, Nalin responded, "I didn't want to wear a suit or plain regular clothes. I wanted to do it the right way. In my mind that was the right way." Nalin adhered to a script of how Indian-Hindu pre-wedding and wedding day events are organized, apparently unaware that the regional and sectarian diversity in India makes a single way of having a Hindu wedding impossible.

We often think the way to resolve competing cultural traditions is by compromising in the middle. Another way is to do both. Although Hamsa and Nalin

67

wanted a traditional Indian-Hindu wedding ceremony followed by an American reception, they instead had a hybrid wedding that drew from three sources of wedding culture: mainstream America, traditional India from the 1960s when the immigrant generation left India, and contemporary Bollywood. In a balancing act to integrate American as well as Indian traditions and customs, Hamsa and Nalin had a culturally and aesthetically-mixed wedding day, as did all the couples I met who had what they described as traditional Hindu weddings. Having led mostly secular lives, occasional Hindus like Hamsa and Nalin were adamant about having traditional weddings. However, despite setting out to have a contrapunctual wedding day with a traditional Indian ceremony followed by an American reception, these couples instead succeeded in having culturally mixed wedding days from start to finish.

Second-generation Indian-American Hindus resist hybridization. Instead of putting on hyphenated Indian-American weddings, they had an Indian-Hindu ceremony followed by an American reception. However, when closely examining Hamsa and Nalin's traditional Indian wedding alongside the wedding festivities of Sachi and Tom which included both a traditional Hindu and a civil ceremony, certain elements of the Hindu ceremony emerge prominently while others fall to the wayside and so, too, with mainstream American wedding customs. Not every element of the Hindu ceremony has the same weight or significance, and this chapter considers which elements of the Hindu wedding ceremony are adapted and thrive in weddings among second-generation Indian-American Hindus, which fall away, and why.

Along with focusing on Hamsa and Nalin as well as Sachi and Tom, I also examine ten other weddings to describe how at weddings of second-generation Indian Americans, three cultures (American, Bollywood, and traditional Indian) collide, demonstrating the hodgepodge of identities second-generation Indian-American Hindus draw from on their wedding day. Nothing is as simple as attributing one custom to expressing symbolic Americanness or Indianness as is the case with Nalin's baraat which gives him the opportunity to express both identities. Instead, the nuances and details of the wedding day festivities combine together to create a fourth flavor of wedding culture in South Asian diasporic studies.

Hamsa's sister greeted Nalin at the entrance of the hotel before leading him to the mandap inside the hall while guests seated themselves according to whether they were on the groom or bride's side. Although Hamsa and Nalin preferred that their guests mix, Hamsa describes them as naturally organizing themselves that way. The guests' sensitivity to sitting on the groom or bride's side is atypical in Indian-Hindu weddings and definitely a result of the mainstream American wedding culture's influence. An obvious example of the influence of American culture in Indian-Hindu weddings is organizational; whereas in India, guests mingle and talk throughout the wedding ceremony, in America they more often than not sit quietly through the ceremony and only begin to mingle after the couple is officially married by the priest.

Waiting for his bride to join him at the mandap, Nalin watched Hamsa while she was carried in a basket down the tulle-decorated wedding aisle. Hamsa describes the experience to me:

> It was great. I felt very excited just to be there, and everyone's clapping, and I kept seeing my friends. Everyone was standing up and co-workers were just amazed that I was being carried in. That's how they do it in Andhra Pradesh.

Hamsa's voice is full of pride when she describes the shock and awe in her guests' faces. Although Hamsa had warned Nalin that her uncles would carry her to the mandap, the image of his bride holding a large coconut as she patiently waited for her uncles to deliver her was awe-inspiring. Naline tells me, "There's no way to be ready for it. It was just incredible."

The success of Mira Nair's *Monsoon Wedding* (2001), a movie set in India that concludes with a traditional Hindu wedding ceremony performed under a stormy monsoon sky, has led many Americans to seek out an authentic Indian wedding that has the chaos and ethnic flair Nair evokes in her film. Couples like Hamsa and Nalin happily accepted the responsibility of entertaining western and Indian guests alike by performing as close to a traditional Hindu wedding as possible. Unfortunately, this strategy backfired for one couple I met. When I asked Ajala how Mitch's Southern Methodist family felt about him possibly having a Hindu wedding ceremony, Ajala explained that his family wanted a Hindu ceremony because they'd seen *Monsoon Wedding*. After the couple decided having a civil ceremony was all they had time to plan in their short engagement, Mitch's family was initially upset that they wouldn't attend a traditional Indian wedding.

Despite Hamsa and Nalin's intention to have a "traditional Hindu" wedding, they adopted many mainstream American customs. For instance, whereas in India there is no formal aisle set aside for the bride to make her way to the mandap (she is usually escorted through throngs of guests), Hamsa created one decorated with tulle, a mainstream American aisle decoration absent from traditional Hindu weddings. Hamsa's walk down the aisle conveys her symbolic ethnic American capital in her otherwise Indian-Hindu wedding ceremony. Still, Hamsa stressed the authenticity of her wedding and reveled in her guests' wonderment at her pure Hindu wedding ceremony.

The baraat, which appealed to three sets of traditions (the traditional Indian one, Bollywood, and American mainstream), and Hamsa's entrance foreshadowed the culturally mixed wedding day festivities. Unlike traditional Indian brides, Hamsa smiled and laughed throughout the ceremony. She said, "I would look up and my friends would wave and smile." Additionally, like eighty percent of the couples I met in my study who had a Hindu wedding ceremony, Hamsa and Nalin hired a priest who could speak English and talk them through the ceremony since having a rehearsal prior to the wedding is not yet part of Indian-American wedding culture and few Indian-American Hindus are familiar with all the elements that make up the larger Hindu wedding ritual. Hamsa and Nalin's English-speaking priest is another example of adaptation in wedding culture among second-generation Indian-American Hindus. Eighty percent of the Hindu weddings I witnessed or saw on video were officiated by an English-speaking priest.

After exchanging garlands, the two were married, and Hamsa, assisted by her sister and cousins, quickly changed out of her pink wedding sari into a regionally traditional red-and-white one before returning to the mandap to sit beside her husband and begin the last portion of the wedding ritual. Non-Hindu guests often interpret the bride and groom's garland exchange as the equivalent to the ring exchange in Judeo-Christian tradition. However, the garland exchange is in fact parallel to when the bride and groom say "I do" in a western American wedding. The garland exchange confirms that each is choosing to marry the other. The pundit and parents of the bride and groom take center stage for most of the ceremony, but in this moment the couple expresses agency and signals the priest to proceed. (Just as pranks are played in mainstream American weddings, they have infiltrated into Hindu ones. For instance, a best man might write the words "HELP ME" on the groom's shoe soles for the congregation to see as he kneels at church. Guests chuckled at Rati and Shiv's ceremony when the groom's best man hung a sign that said "HELP ME" on the back of Shiv's garland.)

Throughout the conclusion of Hamsa and Nalin's ceremony, music played and guests talked freely, frequently approaching the mandap and waving to the couple before joining friends and family in drinking chai (Indian tea) and eating samosas (potato, rice and pea-filled dumplings). The guests were alerted to an auspicious moment in the ceremony when musicians loudly beat their drums. The bride and groom poured rice on each other's head (rice is a symbol of fertility and growth), an element of the South Indian wedding ritual many of the couples I met rejected for their wedding ceremony despite its parallel in American wedding culture of guests throwing rice at the bride and groom as they leave the church. Older women from both families crouched as they whispered blessings in Nalin's ears. The couple did the traditional sapta-padi, where the bride and groom take seven steps, each of which symbolizes a wish for the future together as man and wife. Hamsa betrayed her ignorance of this most sacred element of the Hindu wedding ritual when she said, "I *think* it was seven turns around the fire."

One element of their wedding ritual Nalin and Hamsa were unprepared for, as were all the couples who had Hindu wedding ceremonies, was the wedding band exchange. Nalin and Hamsa were mystified by the game their priest made them play. Their priest placed the platinum wedding bands in a goldfish bowl and instructed the couple to compete with one another to see who could grab a wedding band first. Whoever grabbed a ring two out of three times would be the dominant one in the couple, according to their priest. With guests cheering in the background, Hamsa won. Hamsa says, "I don't think that's a very traditional thing to do I think they added that thing in [the U.S.]." Both were a little confused by the game and expressed regret at the priest's modernization of their wedding ceremony.

Unlike Nalin and Hamsa who were upset with the ring game their priest instructed them to play, Sachi and Tom giggled out of nervousness as well as relief while fishing for their rings during their otherwise serious Hindu wedding ceremony. Hamsa and Nalin were invested in having as authentic and sober a Hindu-

Indian wedding as possible and regretted having to play a game that they deemed as unserious, western, and modern. However, the game is not actually a new invention but an age-old one absent from the second generation's limited body of knowledge regarding Hindu wedding traditions. Second-generation Indian-American Hindus generally deem any element of the ritual that is fun or joyous as inauthentic which says a lot about the second generation's dichotomous views on Indian versus American culture.

One significant characteristic of Hamsa and Nalin's wedding that the couple deemed as authentically "Indian" was their extended family's involvement in the pre-wedding festivities and wedding ceremony. Hamsa's grandmother chose the bride's wedding sari, the bride's uncles carried her down the aisle, and Nalin's aunts gave their blessings. Second-generation Southeast Asians are eager to involve family in their wedding planning and wedding day festivities, even going so far as to staging transnational weddings in India.

Hamsa and Nalin describe their wedding ceremony as designed to adhere to Indian-Hindu wedding tradition whereas the reception was American-style. Hamsa explains, "We'd been to so many weddings at that point, and that's how people have receptions here. I guess we'd just been brainwashed to have American-style receptions." Changing out of her grandmother's hand-picked traditional South Indian wedding sari, Hamsa donned a two-thousand dollar red-and-silver reception sari she had bought in Jackson Heights.

Two of Nalin's friends from college acted as emcees, introducing members from both sides of the family as they made their grand entrance into the reception hall. Despite not having groomsmen at his ceremony, Nalin asked his college friends to wear tuxedos as a way to set them apart from other guests. A close friend gave a slide show of the couple from during their time dating one another, asserting their courtship an American one for anyone who had doubts. Hamsa and Nalin kissed each other in front of their guests, something unusual in receptions of second-generation Indian-American Hindus. When asked if she was embarrassed, Hamsa responds, "We don't embarrass easily." Typically, Indian brides and grooms don't display public affection like holding hands or kissing. However, because Hamsa and Nalin's dating relationship was revealed to the guests through the slide show, the guests summoned the couple to kiss.

Although Hamsa and Nalin were comfortable kissing one another in front of friends and family members, they were torn as to whether they wanted a parents dance. A potentially awkward element in the American wedding reception ritual for second-generation Hindus is the parents dance. Traditionally speaking, Indian parents rarely show public displays of affection for their children, since they are thought to overstep the boundaries between the public and the private. Hamsa describes how she knew her atheist, American-suit-wearing, Beatles-loving father appreciated that opportunity. Nalin admits, "Dancing with my mother was not very traditional."

Just like the Kilis adopted the American mainstream wedding tradition of feeding one another cake, they also integrated the Jewish chair dance into their wedding reception. The couple's friends lifted Hamsa and Nalin, who remained seated in chairs, in the air, shouting and laughing while "Hava Nagila" played in the background. Following the chair dance, Hamsa's younger sister and her friends performed a dance choreographed to a Bollywood hit.

Nalin and Hamsa's wedding was anything but authentic or traditional. It was one that appealed to American, Bollywood, and traditional Indian ideas about what a wedding day should look like. Their South Indian Hindu wedding ritual was preceded by a North Indian Gujurati baraat that appealed to mainstream American, Bollywood and traditional Indian notions about manhood. Hamsa's entrance, while traditional, was along an aisle, an American wedding space absent in Hindu tradition. The couple's priest directed them in English, and Hamsa, rather than act as a demure Indian bride, instead exchanged waves and smiles with her guests.

The reception was a hybrid American-Bollywood one where the bride wore an extravagant sari and the couple revealed their long, American-style courtship with a slide show that concluded with a kiss. Finally, the Beatles, Jewish wedding songs, Indian bhangra and Bollywood film music, were all played and performed at the reception. While from a distance, an observer might say that the couple's wedding ceremony confirmed Hamsa and Nalin's Indian-Hindu background whereas their reception revealed their own ideas about America (affection, dance, play and Western culture), upon closer examination the wedding ceremony and reception do not really appear to be contrapunctual.

Hamsa and Nalin attempted to plan a traditional wedding ceremony while pumping innovation into their reception, but the day's festivities appealed to these three cultures' senses of the wedding. As the day advanced, each element of the ceremony and reception contributed to a tenuous balance of expressing American-ness and connections to India (sometimes a single element expressed both) in an almost schizophrenic conglomeration of wedding cultures.

Sachi and Tom are one of two couples who, unlike Hamsa and Nalin, were totally uninterested in having a traditional Hindu wedding ceremony. Sachi and Tom were also one of a few couples I met who had a civil ceremony on their wedding day. However, even their civil ceremony included religious elements. For example, Tom and Sachi broke the glass, a Jewish custom in wedding ceremonies. Sachi explains how her estranged parents organized and planned her Hindu ceremony and she and Tom designed the civil ceremony:

Everything associated with the civil ceremony, Tom and I planned. My parents were hands off; I picked the officiant, the bridal party, my dress, etc. Planning the civil ceremony was our haven in a way. That was something that just Tom and I had control over and that was important to us. We wanted to structure the whole civil ceremony in a way that was personal. I guess I had been taking notes on weddings all along and was thinking about elements I wanted and didn't want.

Sachi describes her and Tom as picking and choosing customs and traditions that resonated with their values so that the civil ceremony would best fit their personalities and desires. They examined and interrogated wedding traditions such as having a unity candle before deciding to disperse with the custom. Sachi explained, "The idea of having each person light and then blow out the original tapers bothered me."

Sachi's wedding day festivities are an anomaly for many reasons. First of all, she had a tense relationship with her parents. The emotional anguish her parents caused Sachi functioned to distance her from Indian culture and Hindu traditions because she saw both as sources of their idiosyncrasies. Sachi was the only bride I met who invested nothing in having a traditional or authentic Indian wedding. Instead she expressed her connection with mainstream American culture by wearing a white Vera Wang wedding gown and planning a distinctly American wedding reception. While her parents planned the couple's traditional Hindu wedding ceremony, Sachi ignored modern-day Bollywood India and organized a traditionally American reception instead.

As a result of not having any interest in a Hindu wedding ceremony and partying the previous night with her bridesmaids, Sachi can recount little of what happened during her Hindu wedding ceremony which was conducted early in the morning on her wedding day. She said, "I'd only gotten three hours of sleep so I have no idea what really happened." The couple had an abridged, ninety-minute long Hindu wedding ceremony conducted by what Sachi calls "a mercenary priest." She explains: "He was a priest unattached to institutions and performs ceremonies other priests won't. He usually marries religiously mixed couples." Although the priest conducted the ceremony in Hindi, he quietly translated himself for Tom to understand.

Following South Indian tradition, Sachi's uncles carried her to the mandap. She describes how the basket tilted because her stronger uncles were carrying her on one side and her weaker uncles were carrying her from the other side. She tells me: "My brother was trying to stabilize me from behind. I think the tradition is all well and good for the will-o'-the-wisp brides of yore," Sachi said disconcertedly while describing the experience. The voluminous sari she wore and her struggle to balance herself in the basket made her feel like a "fat bride," unlike Hamsa who glowed with happiness when describing her grand entrance.

At the mandap, Tom and Sachi were separated from seeing each other by a curtain of silk. (The silk curtain is an ancient remnant of Hindu tradition whereby the wedding was often the first time the bride and groom met one another as a consequence of having an arranged marriage.) Once lifted, Tom and Sachi were officially married, thus separating the bride and groom with silk is an element of the Hindu wedding ritual that has survived immigration and the dominant American wedding culture because of its parallel to the mainstream American tradition of lifting a bride's veil. Tom describes how lifting the antarpatha, or silk curtain, was "like the lifting of the veil I could finally see her."

One aspect of South Indian weddings Hamsa and Nalin happily integrated into their ceremony but that Tom and Sachi and other couples were hesitant about or rejected was pouring rice on each other's heads. Tom tells me what the couple calls the "Rice Story": "For weeks before the wedding she was telling me how part of the ceremony involved pouring rice on one another's head. She insisted that I be careful not to ruin her hair. 'Don't dump the rice,' she told me. When it came time for her she was not as careful. She dumped all the rice in my hair. I thought that was pretty funny, after all she said." Couples like Samir and Salila, rather than risk ruining the bride's carefully-coifed hair, instead rejected the tradition. Salila explained, "When I have make-up on and look pretty I don't want rice thrown on me." Samir, Salila's husband, admitted to me in private that, "In my opinion [the rice aspect of the ritual] was the most significant reason why we didn't have a Telugu ceremony."

For some brides such as Salila, displaying her femininity was at the forefront of planning her wedding. She described how important it was to her that she feel "like a princess" which was why she was adamant about choosing her own lengha to wear at the reception and refused to let her husband pour rice in her hair since it would spoil her professionally-styled hair. Whereas traditionally, Hindu brides are expected to put aside vanity and bend to the conventions of a traditional wedding ritual, American brides such as Salila desired to remain at the center of attention and look suitable for the role. Although some couples (like Hamsa and Nalin) relied on scripted traditions in planning their wedding, the vast majority of couples interrogated every element of the Hindu wedding ritual before deciding which to integrate and which to reject. Whereas Hamsa and Nalin were adamant about having a traditional religious ceremony, couples like Salila and Samir based their decision not to have a South Indian ceremony on Salila's refusal to have her hair ruined.

While guests tasted the assortment of Indian and American hors d'oeuvres at the cocktail hour, Sachi changed into her white Vera Wang wedding gown for her civil ceremony. In an effort to distance herself from her family and what she called Indian values, Sachi wore a white wedding gown to the civil ceremony and walked unescorted down an aisle while a string quartet performed ceremonial music Tom composed. Sachi rejected being escorted down the aisle by their father as a way to assert independence and to distance herself from the traditional patriarchal values expressed in the custom. Kanyadan, the analog to a father walking his daughter down an aisle in the Hindu wedding ritual, was rejected by brides such as Chandana who were uninterested in participating in what she deemed as an antiquated and misogynistic tradition.

During Sachi and Tom's civil ceremony, a close friend from college sang and another read from Kahlil Gibran's *The Prophet*. Columbia University's chaplain, whom Sachi described as a "wonderful, erudite African-American female Christian minister," officiated, giving a Biblically-based sermon that "was also very open." Tom and Sachi included the Jewish custom of "breaking the glass" but with a modern twist. Rather than have Tom break the glass, Sachi placed her foot on top of Tom's, and they both broke the glass together. Sachi explained, "Symbolically, it was meant to show we are united." When I asked Tom why he chose this custom for his civil ceremony, he explains:

Breaking the glass was a nod to my [Jewish] mother, but it is also an interesting symbol. Some people interpret it as the destruction of the second temple. Others interpret it as the fragility of life and marriage but then I'm not sure why you'd want to break it. Breaking the glass symbolizes the irrevocability of it. Once you break the glass you can't put it back together again. Some things can't be undone.

Sachi kissed Tom before all their family and friends. Like many of her peers, kissing her husband in front of family made Sachi feel uncomfortable. Almost all the second-generation Indian-American Hindu women I met grew up with traditional Indian notions of womanhood and being a bride, including acting demurely and virginal, pure and without sensuality.

The couple followed their Hindu and civil ceremonies with a western style reception that included the couple's first dance. When asked if she felt nervous about dancing with Tom in front of all the guests, she replied, "It was silly not to have rehearsed the first dance," and made no further comment. Sachi did not have a father-daughter dance because she felt that it would be awkward. The couple hired a jazz quartet; Bollywood and bhangra music were not part of Sachi's wedding reception, but to the delight of Tom's side of the family, the band played "Hava Nagila" with a jazzy melody.

Sachi's mother gave a toast, something unexpected in both Hindu and American weddings. Often, the bride's father welcomes the guests, followed by toasts by the best man and maid of honor. Sachi's mother's toast more closely resembled a bidhai, an ancient Hindu custom where the bride's mother, sisters, cousins and girlfriends gather together in a solemn farewell to the bride. Sachi says, "My mom gave a long speech. I had no idea it was happening. She spent a long time talking about the pain of separation and she was crying. I was a little stunned. I felt like she should be talking about being happy, not pain. I later understood how she must have felt." Although none of the brides I met had a traditional bidhai at their weddings, as it is no longer difficult to travel to see one's newly-married sister or daughter in the modern age of planes, trains, and automobiles, Sachi's mother's mournful speech captures the sentiments behind the bidhai in a socially acceptable form appropriate for western-style reception and a mixed crowd.

Sachi and Tom's wedding was one of two that didn't draw from the three wedding cultures that dominate the second generation's wedding planning: romantic and modern Bollywood, traditional India from when the immigrant generation left the country, and mainstream America. Just as the majority of the brides and grooms I met used their wedding day as a forum to express their Indian background and Hindu religious identity at their ceremony as well as their Americanness at their reception, Sachi and Tom designed their civil ceremony to convey their American values and tastes and to distance themselves from Sachi's parents, whose conservative and religious temperaments created friction in their relationships with Sachi.

Elements of the Hindu Wedding

Although Sachi and Tom had a religious Hindu ceremony, they performed it without elements such as the kanyadan where the father gives away his daughter. Here

I describe which elements of pre-wedding and wedding-day Hindu tradition have been embraced, adapted, rejected, and why. For instance, in the previous chapter I describe how the mendhi party thrives in America because this make-up symbolizes a woman's status as a bride and because the party performs the practical function of introducing young girls to Hindu wedding tradition. On the wedding day, the baraat, the spectacle of a groom arriving at the wedding ceremony on a horse, is a popular tradition among second-generation Indian-American Hindus because it appeals to three wedding cultures upon which Indian Americans draw: Bollywood, traditional India, and mainstream America. A groom who arrives on a horse to his wedding is an age-old tradition that also conveys romance and chivalry, two values embraced in Bollywood and mainstream American wedding culture. Additionally, the baraat is analogous to the white limousine in mainstream America which is seen as a lavish method of transport for a couple on their wedding day.

Elements of the wedding ceremony such as holding a silk curtain so the bride and groom can't see each other, exchanging garlands, and performing the sapta-padi, have all been embraced by second-generation Indian-American Hindus as a consequence of having analogs in mainstream American wedding tradition as well as the fact that those customs, by putting India on display, allow second-generation Indian-American Hindus to exhibit their ethnic-American identity. One example is the curtain of silk that separates the bride and groom. After this curtain is lifted, the couple is considered married and thus begins the conclusion of the ceremony. Tom likened the silk curtain to lifting a veil, an analog that no doubt helps this element of Hindu wedding tradition to survive.

Another element that has been embraced is the varmala, or garland exchange. Although it does not literally translate into "I do," varmala is a non-verbal agreement between the bride and groom that they choose one another to marry, the only time the couple shows agency in a traditional Hindu ceremony. By placing garlands around one another's necks, the couple expresses free choice, an American value, even as it allows the couple to express Indianness. The couple enters into a social contract when it exchanges garlands by uniting two formerly separate families.

Finally, the sapta-padi is an element of the Hindu wedding ceremony integrated into all the Hindu ceremonies I observed. This is likely because the ancient image of an Indian-dressed bride and groom walking around a fire is the core of a Hindu wedding and visually symbolizes traditional Hindu weddings to both outsiders and Indian Hindus. The sapta-padi expresses the unequivocally eastern and ancient origin of the ceremony and the religion. Although spoken vows are non-existent in Hindu wedding ceremonies (the couple never speaks), each step around the sacred fire signifies a vow each makes to the other. In other words, the sapta-padi is a popular element of the Hindu wedding ceremony among the second generation because it allows the couple to have it both ways: to express their agency while following a traditional wedding ceremony rotted in customs of arranged marriage. Like the baraat, the sapta-padi confirms the couple's ethnic-American identity.

Rati and Shiv's wedding program describes for their guests the significance of the sapta-padi:

First:	Together, we will live through happiness and sorrow.
Second:	Together, we will respect our culture and traditions of our family.
Third:	Together, we will always listen to each other and speak with kindness and patience.
Fourth:	Together, we will support each other through good times and bad times.
Fifth:	Together, we will remain faithful to one another.
Sixth:	Together, we will always be honest to each other.
Seventh:	Together, we will help fulfill each other's aspirations and perform religious rites.

Each step carries significance for what marriage means to the couple and to the community. The sentiments are reminiscent of those spoken in vows by a bride and groom in a Judeo-Christian ceremony. The sapta-padi echoes the notion that the couple must live with each other for better or for worse, in sickness and in health with the first step where the bride and groom vow to live through happiness and sorrow. The vow to honor and respect you in the white wedding ceremony finds its place in the third step of the sapta-padi where the couple promises to speak with kindnesss and patience. The fourth step of the sapta-padi reflects the Judeo-Christian vow that the couple remains one unit through good times and bad times. The fifth and sixth steps pledge absolute monogamy and honesty, two values which are also expressed in the typical American wedding ceremony when the couple vows to be faithful partners. Only the second and seventh steps of the sapta-padi have no direct correlation to the American wedding vows. In mainstream America, where the younger generation often lives a very secular life, vows rarely contain promises to continue cultural traditions or participate in longstanding religious rites.

Mainstream American Wedding Culture

Whereas elements of the Hindu wedding ceremony are partially embraced because they have analogs in mainstream American Judeo-Christian weddings and because they put India on display, second-generation Indian-American Hindus integrate American wedding customs if they have significance that is meaningful in Indian culture or because they serve a practical function. The Indian Americans I met come from means; the combination of modern technology, resources and wealth make it easy for second-generation Indian-American Hindus to adapt both mainstream American and Indian wedding customs. Practically-speaking, although Hamsa's tulle-decorated aisle drew from American wedding culture and expressed her subscription to American wedding tradition, the space allowed her to prominently display her symbolic ethnic Indian capital for all her guests to witness.

Along with the bride walking down an aisle, a popular element of mainstream American wedding tradition embraced by Indian-American Hindus is having a bridal party and groomsmen. Having a wedding party is a way for second-generation Indian-American Hindus to convey Indian culture's community-based values. It also allows friends to participate in wedding day festivities. Ajay described his wedding as a Hindu wedding with elements of the Christian wedding because he and Sonia had groomsmen and bridesmaids. Additionally, Ajay and Sonia were the only couple I met who had a rehearsal, a custom that has not infiltrated wedding culture among second-generation Indian-American Hindus probably because so much time and money is spent orchestrating Indian pre-wedding events such as the mendhi party or religious engagement party.

Although walking down an aisle and having a wedding party were popular American customs adopted by second-generation Indian-American Hindus, perhaps the most widespread element of the mainstream American wedding embraced by second-generation Indian-American Hindus and their parents is the wedding program. Hindu weddings in India are often described as chaotic; the wedding usually includes a large group of guests reuniting with friends and family, business associates and acquaintances, as they partake in refreshment and chi. In the United States, second-generation Indian-American Hindus have adopted the organization of the American wedding.

Part of this organization is the wedding program which functions to not only frame the elements of the ceremony as they happen but also educate non-Hindu guests about the ceremony they are about to witness. In India and among the immigrant generation, the meaning of the elements that make up the Hindu ceremony is not as important as performing them. However, second-generation Indian-American Hindus I met emphasized the significance of various customs partly because they deemed them characteristically Indian. Ironically, the adaptation of the Judeo-Christian wedding program expresses identification with a mainstream American wedding tradition yet its purpose (as a way to instruct non Hindus about the significance of the elements that make up a Hindu wedding) functions to display ties to Hinduism. In one instance, having a wedding program (which is not a tradition in Hindu wedding planning in India), rather than enhance a couple's ethnic-American identity, instead worked against it: Kamini described how her blended ceremony to Jason, an Episcopalian, looked Indian, but the program looked Christian because all the Bible verses were spelled out.

Up until now I've described components of the mainstream American wedding ceremony that have been embraced by the couples I met. Perhaps the most contested element of the American wedding ritual among Indian-American Hindu couples is the kiss. Indian immigrants that left India in the 1960s and 1970s have not experienced modern day India where romantic and modern Bollywood has a presence in daily life and the country has evolved towards modernity. The immigrant generation has indoctrinated its children into a culture where public displays of affection are unacceptable. Only one couple I met incorporated the wedding kiss into their Hindu ceremony. Salila explains, "We had a love marriage so we kissed throughout the day." Unlike Salila, Ajay and Sonia described the wedding kiss as going against Indian custom, expressing the second generation's association of conservative values with India and romance with America, a simple and dichotomous worldview that ignores Bollywood India, a culture they drew from when planning their wedding day festivities. (To this day, Ajay and Sonia refrain from holding hands in front of their families even though they are married). Only one couple in my study incorporated the kiss into the Hindu wedding ceremony. Jason was adamant that he kiss his bride whereas Kamini was hesitant. Jason tells me, "The kiss is not scripturally mandated, but it's not a wedding until you've kissed the bride, so I was insistent on that." He recalls how up until the wedding day he would threaten to dip Kamini. She joked that if he did she would take him straight to divorce court.

Another element of the mainstream American wedding that is not popular among second-generation Indian-American Hindus is reciting vows. Only two of twenty couples recited vows at their wedding ceremony, one couple at their blended Hindu-Episcopalian ceremony and the other at their civil ceremony. One reason why reciting vows is unpopular among second-generation Indian-American Hindu couples is because reciting vows, like the kiss, is a public display of affection, an act which is not considered appropriate by the immigrant generation who left India before the country westernized. Additionally, reciting vows places the bride and groom at the center of their wedding ceremony which is not in keeping with Hindu wedding customs. Finally, the couple does not traditionally express agency in the ceremony; exchanging vows demonstrates agency, a value that seems out of place in a traditional Hindu ceremony. In one touching yet hilariously ignorant instance, the justice-of-the-peace who officiated Ajala and Mitch's civil ceremony attempted to inject the couple's ceremony with Indian culture by reciting an Indian wedding prayer she found on Google. Weeks after the wedding, Ajala researched the prayer and found out that it was an Apache Indian one rather than one from the subcontinent.

Contrary to Hindu wedding tradition, Savita played a pivotal role in organizing her wedding. At Savita and Dev's wedding, the bride emceed when she welcomed her guests and introduced friends and family members. The couple's vows, though sincere, were sentimental, bordering on self-promotion. Dev recognized Savita's work with domestic violence and her political activism as well as her "romantic and searching side." He used their love for the tabla as a metaphor for their relationship: "I feel like our relationship is very much like something we saw the night we first met: the call and response that takes place in Indian classical music between an instrument and the drum." Although the couple had a civil ceremony, Savita's vows alluded to Hinduism when she said,

If God had come down and offered me the one boon of creating a perfect mate for me, I would have felt greedy asking for all that I have in you. I can't be presumptuous as to know the intensions of God, but I would like to think that your soul is one of the ones that mine travels with [in keeping with reincarnation], if I don't marry you now, you'll catch up with me eventually.

Savita concluded the ceremony with a kiss. Savita later explained why she and Dev took such lengths to talk during their ceremony. She said, "Usually the wedding is about family and guests. It was important that at my wedding I speak and my husband speak. We wanted to state why we were marrying. It wasn't a contract between two families. It was a contract between us." Savita and Dev's ceremony, unlike all the other weddings in this study emphasized the couple over their families and community.

Rejecting Elements of the Hindu Ceremony

In addition to largely rejecting elements of the mainstream American wedding ceremony such as exchanging vows and sealing the ceremony with a kiss, couples I met also interrogated and sometimes rejected components of the traditional Hindu wedding ceremony. For Chandana, unlike the majority of the other brides I met, it was important that the religious aspects of her Hindu ceremony reflect her value system. In the process of researching her wedding program (she copied and pasted text from various Indian wedding websites onto a Word document), she learned about the significance of each element of the Hindu ceremony and realized that there were customs that conflicted with her beliefs. Chandana tells me, "Jews and Christians grapple with religious texts and scriptures, but you just don't see that among Hindus of our generation." Researching her wedding ceremony inspired Chandana to consider a reform movement in Hinduism. She described how Hindu priests would not sit and work with her on the ceremony. She added, "Our priest had a real problem with cutting out some of these pieces." Chandana, however, was adamant. She said, "If I was going to have a Hindu ceremony, I wanted it to be meaningful to me and not do it blindly."

Elements of Hindu wedding rituals survived immigration and time only if adapted to contemporary values. Whether an element of the Hindu wedding ceremony had a practical function or an analog in mainstream wedding culture largely determined if it was rejected by second-generation Indian-American Hindus planning their wedding day. Only two out of the twenty couples began their wedding with the kasi yatra, a predominantly South Indian ceremony where the groom threatens to go to Kashi in the Hamsalayas and refuses to marry the bride. The bride's family must then go through the motions of pleading with the groom and offering to bribe him back with gifts. Although Ravi's family is North Indian, they embraced this tradition after researching and discussing the custom with Supriya's South Indian grandmother (who made sure Ravi understood what was expected of him).

Supriya described how happy she was to include a custom in her wedding so traditional that even her parents did not participate in it at their wedding in India. In Satish and Sapna's wedding, Satish put on the pretense of leaving which Sapna's father and brother responded to by coaxing him into staying. Everyone, including the groom and his soon-to-be-father-in-law, was smiling. Sapna's uncle gave a garland with yellow, pink and white flowers to Satish for staying and marrying his niece. While these two couples willingly played along and performed the custom, the majority of the men and women I met criticized the kasi yatra as an outdated custom.

Another contested element of the Hindu wedding ceremony is one traditional North Indian wedding ceremonies where the groom's eyes are shielded from viewing the bride. Prior to meeting Sonia at the mandap, Ajay's family placed on his head a turban, or sehra, which he described as too tight. He was vaguely aware that he might have to wear a turban at his wedding, but he was caught off guard when relatives tried to fasten a silver mukut, or crown, on the turban to cover his eyes. As part of the serabandi custom, the groom is supposed to cover his eyes prior to seeing his wife for the first time. During the ongoing match between Ajay and his family, Ajay was adamant that he wouldn't wear the sera whereas his family focused on maintaining the tradition. They did not understand how Ajay could agree to a traditional Hindu wedding yet refuse to wear the sera. The idea of embracing elements of the Hindu wedding ceremony while rejecting others was not something they could easily digest. Ajay later explained that he did not think he would like how the pictures would look and was "uncomfortable with that level of tradition."

The kanyadan is another highly-contested element of the Hindu wedding ceremony that many brides I met rejected. Although the kanyadan has its analog in the white wedding where the father-of-the-bride escorts his daughter and gives her away, only two out of the twenty brides I met integrated this element into their wedding ceremony. In the kanyadan, the father-of-the-bride places his daughter's hand on the groom's, and the priest recites Sanskrit verses that describe the significance of the hand-off. Salila, one of the two brides who had the kanyadan, said she never understood why brides cried at their wedding. She added: "But I cried through the whole ceremony like a baby." The kanyadan element of the ceremony provoked Salila the most. According to Samir, her husband, the priest was "pouring it on really hard but it was helpful in a way because we really understood the significance of what we were doing." When her father placed her hand in Samir's hand, the priest translated into English the significance of that action for Salila to understand. Salila tells me, "Sometimes it's much nicer when they don't translate everything. I started balling for ten minutes. My mother had to call my sisters to [the mandap] to give me tissues After the ceremony my photographer told me to go and change and re-do my make-up. My entire make-up was running."

Customs are more sustainable if they make cultural as well as practical sense. The bidhai, another element of the Hindu wedding ceremony rejected by all but one couple in this study, was seen as impractical, with no significance in modern American society. Originally created for when the bride married off and left her village, the bidhai is a melodramatic and tearful goodbye. Supriya's family was the only one that staged a bidhai, but even hers was modified. Supriya refused to cry and asked her deejay not to play somber music. Instead, her farewell was joyous rather than tearful. For an element of the Hindu wedding ceremony to remain alive, it has to adapt by resonating with contemporary culture. Second-generation brides can't relate to the village Indian woman whose time spent with her family is dramatically cut back after marrying; so the bidhai articulates a tension that is no longer there. Rather than strengthening the second generation's image of community, family ties and commitment to cultural continuity, the mournful nature of a traditional bidhai simply focuses guests' attention on the somber and unnecessary spectacle of women crying.

The Indian-American Wedding Reception

The least-contested element of the wedding day, according to second-generation Indian-American Hindus I met, is the reception. An elegant yet non-verbal compromise has been crafted over the last forty years between the first and second generations regarding how to stage an Indian-American wedding reception. Although the bride's parents paid for nineteen of twenty of the weddings in my study, the first generation plans the ceremony and the second generation plans the reception. The second generation does not assert independence, a characteristically American value, by offering to pay for their own wedding; almost universally the American-born Hindus expected their parents to pay.

As Samir put it, "The cultural aspect [of the reception] was the dressing, but the bulk of the planning was around ensuring that the guests would enjoy themselves. Culture was just how we dressed up the cake. Ultimately it was an American reception with an Indian cap." The reception is often the first and only time on the wedding day when the bride wears wedding clothes of her own choice. Her steadfast decision to choose her own reception outfit expresses values such as independence and adulthood as well as her American upbringing. Wearing a self-chosen reception outfit also symbolizes the second generation's intention to have a reception that more closely fits its way of life as modern urban professionals living or working in New York. Men like Nalin and Tom changed out of their kurtas and into tuxedos and suits, suggesting that the men, too, are vested in looking and feeling their best at their receptions.

Receptions more closely resemble that of American-style wedding receptions because the second generation takes center stage. The wedding reception is a place where second-generation Indian-American Hindus display their American roots after participating in an Indian-Hindu wedding ceremony. Whereas the priest and both sets of parents are often central figures on the mandap and the couple dutifully follows their instructions, at the reception, the couple and their friends dominate.

For example, Ajay and Sonia walked hand-in-hand as they made their way to the center of the dance floor, accompanied by groomsmen and bridesmaids. The best man made a speech and all the bridesmaids shared a few words. The couple then gave thanks to their guests. Ajay and Sonia's thank you speech, although customary in American weddings, violates the couple's function as mere accessories in traditional Hindu weddings.

At Hamsa and Nalin's reception, one friend conducted a slide show of photographs from their courtship, a form of reception entertainment clearly adopted from the mainstream American receptions since dating before marriage is not publicly discussed and thus should not be advertised among Indians. The slide show functioned to challenge the stereotypes of pre-modern India's arranged marriage model which is stigmatized in America.

Whereas a kiss between the groom and bride has no place in the traditional Hindu wedding ceremony, the kiss that is meant to seal the deal in mainstream American Judeo-Christian wedding ceremonies usually takes place during the modern wedding reception. For couples that were too shy to integrate a wedding kiss into their ceremony and who expressed horror at the idea of a nearby grandparent witnessing this immodest display, the reception was a forum in which traditional Indian decorum could be safely ignored. In fact, Bollywood's influence in the dress, music, and dance aspects of a second-generation Hindu's reception also legitimizes the couple's kiss at their reception. Bollywood's eastern roots and western values facilitate a way for second-generation Indian-American Hindus to express both Americanness and Indianness at their wedding reception.

Four of the wedding receptions I attended included the Jewish chair dance even when it was a pure Hindu couple who had just married. Having seen the Jewish chair dance in numerous movies and television shows, the first and second generations view it as a distinctly American wedding reception tradition and have adopted it for their own receptions, illuminating how fluid is the line between American and immigrant traditions in a nation composed almost entirely of immigrant stock. Whereas for couples such as Tom and Sachi where one person was Jewish the chair dance was a natural component of the reception, couples like Hamsa and Nalin also participated in this rite. The chair dance, in second-generation Indian-American wedding culture, is thought of as expressing an American identity rather than Jewishness, much like the participants equated getting married under a mandap or the sapta-padi component of their ceremony as Indian rather than Hindu. Over and over again, the twenty couples I met thought in terms of culture and ethnicity rather than religion and faith.

Finally, Bollywood India played a big role in the design of the American-style reception. The women universally wore Indian clothes, usually lenghas, which often resemble a costume out of a Bollywood film. Indian food such as chicken korma and basmati rice was served and party favors such as mithai (Indian sweets) were distributed among the guests. Indian music played a large role in coloring the American-style reception as Indian; often, DJs were told to play Bollywood songs. Young guests could gyrate to the pure Indian sounds coming out of modern Bollywood without having to worry about the wrath of their immigrant parents who were overjoyed by this exhibition of Indian culture.

Playing Bollywood music, dancing to Bollywood film songs, and wearing Bollywood-style clothing were ways in which second-generation Indian-American Hindus could pay homage to their Indian heritage while expressing what they conceived of as western values (joy, youth, and sensuality). Thus, Bollywood India emerged in my study as the third culture which straddles modern America and traditional. Bollywood India served as a culture from which my participants could claim both their modern-day American values as well as strong ties to India without reproach from the first generation or their white, mainstream American peers.

An easy way to keep the reception from diverting too much from the Indian ceremony that usually precedes it is by playing Indian film and bhangra music. Often a family friend or young sister will perform an Indian dance for guests. Kirti's family friend danced to "Kalyanji Anandji," a famous Bollywood film song that has also become a popular bhangra workout musical track. In the mostly American receptions, Bollywood songs represent India too, even though the tunes point to how radically India has evolved ever since the immigrant generation left the country. But rather than see Bollywood's movies as a conglomeration of eastern and western cultures, second-generation Indian-American Hindus view it as an authentic source of Indian culture from which to draw in staging an ethnic Indian wedding and reception. Although choreography in Indian films include steamy moves not without the occasional gyration, the music's ethnic origins legitimizes the dance style and gives it a certain authenticity that allows the second generation to enjoy it without the fear of lessening their perceived connection to traditional Indian culture or disgruntling their parents.

In South India, neither alcohol nor meat is served at wedding receptions, and dancing is not customary, but all the South Indian couples I met served alcohol and meat and danced at their receptions. Often, couples and their Indian parents saw the Hindu ceremony as a forum to express Indian tradition and the reception as a place to express ethnic Americanness. A significant way to maintain the Indian flavor at the otherwise American wedding reception is by serving Indian food. However, non-Indian food was also served at a few receptions; Kamini and Jason's reception offered a little bit of something for everyone: Indian cuisine, seafood and Mexican dishes. Ajala and Mitch offered not only steak and salmon at their reception but also chicken korma, a distinctly North Indian dish, while another bicultural couple offered wedding cake to guests but sent them home with methai as a party favor. Displaying and offering ethnic objects such as Indian food and party favors enhanced the ethnic flavor of a reception during an otherwise American wedding reception.

Even mainstream American reception decorations like having an ice sculpture were embraced by second-generation Indian-American Hindus. Kirti, rather than display an ice sculpture of a swan or a heart, instead had one of Ganesha, the elephant-headed god of good fortune (Figure 10). Sapna's Indian caterer created a sea-foam green cake to match her reception lengha, complete with a cake topper that looked remarkably like Sapna and Satish. Shaadi Presentations, an Indian wedding planning company, specializes in making wedding cake toppers that represent the couple in their wedding clothes. Sapna sent the vendor photographs of her sea foam green lengha and Satish's Nehru suit, and Shaadhi Presentations turned around their request in a matter of weeks. Wedding props such as the ice sculpture and cake topper that would otherwise be considered components of a mainstream American wedding reception instead are adapted to express the couple's ethnic-American identity.

Half of the brides I met integrated fun games like the bouquet toss into their receptions. Ajala explained how tossing her bouquet was a way to inject her otherwise ethnically-flavored wedding with a western tradition familiar to her husband Mitch's family. All the couples I met had a first dance with their spouse and only three brides felt comfortable enough to dance with their father at their wedding reception. Unlike in Indian weddings, men and women alike were asked to make toasts. Ajala describes how her mother "wanted to turn the reception into C-SPAN. She wanted lots of people to speak including my great uncle and my godfather." In many of the weddings I attended respected family members like the grandfather or great uncle gave lengthy speeches despite the fact that they were peripheral figures in the bride and groom's lives.

Conclusion

The ultimate expression of one's Indian and Hindu cultural background *and* American roots, symbolic ethnic Indian and American capital, is staging an Indian-Hindu wedding. My interviews of twenty couples and participant observation of their Indian-American Hindu weddings led me to conclude that the community has evolved enough in the last forty years to have established a pre-arranged wedding culture which embraces components of both the mainstream American and Indian-Hindu wedding ceremony and reception. Whereas the first generation organizes the Hindu ceremony, their children coordinate the American-style reception. Instead of choosing either India or America, this community embraces both cultures in the search for a spouse, marriage proposal, and wedding planning.

This both/and model for wedding planning is reflective of the community's marriage market where a competitive spousal candidate has both symbolic ethnic Indian and American capital. Likewise, finding a spouse that meets both Indian-Hindu and mainstream-American standards of success is reflected in the community's marriage market, engagement and wedding culture. The arranged meeting model for marriage draws from both pre-modern India's arranged marriage and America's love marriage. Arranged meetings take into account religious, language and regional compatability before dating commences with the intent of love and marriage.

This both/and model finds its way into the engagement ritual. U.S-born Hindus are expected to participate in both American and Indian-Hindu engagement rituals. A public engagement centered around puja (prayer) is an opportunity for the couple to accrue symbolic ethnic Indian capital, a term I employ to describe a quality of a person when they act, speak, or dress in an Indian manner. I use the term occasional Hindus to describe the second generation as displaying their Hindu religious background at rites-of-passage such as the marriage proposal and wedding day.

Bollywood, whose Indian origin grants it authenticity and whose emphasis on romance accommodates American values, is the mediating third culture around which the community applies the both/and model to wedding planning. Elements of the Hindu ceremony that are adapted have analogs in Judeo-Christian weddings, put India on display, serve a practical function, and accommodate contemporary values.

The both/and model reinforces the community's identity as ethnic-American as well as confirms that success in America is because of, rather than despite, their religious background and cultural heritage. Producing an Indian wedding like one would a movie, with props such as the red wedding sari, the flower-encrusted mandap, and methai party favors, is the ultimate way in which second-generation Indian-American Hindus and their families demonstrate their success.

The second-generation Indian-Hindu American's wedding functions to not only publicly display idealized Indian-Hindu culture but also to create a formal forum for the second generation to act out its ethnic-American identity. The Hindu wedding ceremony is meant to convey the second-generation's resistance to cultural dilution while at the same time embracing American culture and values.

By having an Indian Hindu wedding, this generation touts its ethnic heritage and faith in the Hindu wedding ceremony and embraces the American mainstream secular daily lifestyle at their reception. However, staging a Hindu-Indian wedding also aligns the second generation with what being American is and what it can be. In staging the customs of their family's ancestors, the second generation proves how being American is part and parcel of adopting and keeping Old World traditions alive, and that being American does not exclude being Indian. The second generation's innocence of their own use of American, Bollywood and traditional Indian culture in planning their weddings suggests their lack of awareness that cultures evolve and interact with one another. In second-generation Indian-American Hindu wedding culture, a third, hybrid culture inspired by Bollywood is emerging. This new creation demonstrates how customs, traditions and elements of ritual survive immigration and time through adaptation, their ability to display ethnicity, and practical relevance.

Glossary

aarthi	form of worship using lit candles
Abu Jani-Sandeep Khosla	team of Indian fashion designers
aerogram	airmail letter
Aishwarya Rai	famous Bollywood actress and model
Amitabh Bachan	one of the most famous Bollywood actors to have ever lived
Andhra Pradesh	a state in South India
Apache Indians	Britain-based desi rap group
Archana Kochar	Indian fashion designer
arranged marriage	traditional model for marriage in pre-modern India when a man and woman met for the first time at their wedding to one another
arranged meetings	second-generation Indian-American Hindus are introduced to other ethnically and religiously compatible men and women who constitute a pool of prospective spouses to choose from
authentic ethnicity	what Dr. Kibria describes as the operation of race as an identity marker, legitimate rather than contrived or fake.
baarat	marriage procession where the bridegroom travels to the wedding site accompanied by family and friends
bajaans	religious songs that celebrate the love of God
baraat	a procession of friends and family who lead the groom sitting on a horse to the wedding hall
Benzer	a high-end, Mumbai-based clothing store that sells women and men's clothing
beti	Hindi word for daughter
Bhagavad Gita	ancient Sanskrit text

bhangra	name for a lively dance and the music that accompanies this type of dance
bharatanatyam	classical Indian dance
Bibi	Indian fashion magazine aimed at non-resident Indians that focuses on wedding planning
bidhai	melodramatic and tearful goodbye at the conclusion of a wedding between the bride and her female family and friends
bindi	a bride's forehead is embellished with tikka/bindi which run on top of both sides of the eye-brows
bio-data	matrimonial resume that includes information such as income, level of education, regional origin, and language fluency
Bollywood	the name for India's film industry
brahmacharya	the student stage of life
Brahmins	highest and most prestigious caste in India
Brain Drain	term used to describe the emigration of trained and talented individuals from India to America in the 1960s and '70s
Bride and Prejudice	Gurinder Chadha's 2004 movie starring Aishwarya Rai
bridezilla	term used to describe an engaged woman obsessed with planning her wedding
caste	ancient system in India of social stratification
chai	Indian tea
chicken korma	chicken curry
chicken tikka masala	baked chicken marinated in spices
choli	midriff-baring blouse worn underneath a sari
cultural Hindus	Raymond Brady Williams' description of Hindus for whom their religion is a group of customs and moral principles
desi	slang word for an ethnic Indian
Devdas	popular Bollywood film released in 2002
dhoti	white fabric wrapped around a mans waist usually worn by South Indian Hindu grooms
diaspora	an ethnic population dispersed throughout the world
dosas	South Indian potato dish
dowry	gift of money and/or valuables given to the groom and his family by the bride's parents

Dulhan Expo	where Indian wedding vendors congregate and market their bridal fashion, decorations and wedding services to South Asian women
dupatta	long scarf worn over a lengha or sari
F.O.B.	slang word used for a recent immigrant (fresh off the boat)
first generation	immigrant generation
Ganesh/Ganesha	elephant-headed god of good fortune
garba	form of dancing
grahastha	householder stage
Gujarat	state in Western India
henna	dye used for body art
immigrant generation	first generation
India Abroad	Khandelwal describes it as the first Indian newspaper produced by the immigrant generation
Indian Institute of Technology	widely known as the best university in India
Jackson Heights, Queens	Indian ghetto in Queens, New York
Jhumpa Lahiri	popular Indian-American fiction writer
ji	suffix used as a mark of respect
kanya pravesh	where the bride is escorted to the mandap by a maternal uncle
kanyadan	where the bride's father places his daughter's right hand in the groom's right hand as a sign of giving her away
kasi yatra	South-Indian Hindu element of the wedding ritual where the groom threatens to abandon his bride on her wedding day
Kerala	state in South India
Krishna	the highest god in Hinduism
kufi skull cap	cap worn by religious Muslim men
kurta	a traditional Indian mans outfit made up of loose pajama pants and a matching tunic
Lagan	popular Bollywood film released in 2005
Lakshmi	goddess of wealth
lengha	modern-day skirt and fitted-top ensemble for young women
love marriage	modern American model for marriage where two people marry because they are in love with each other
Madhuri Dixit	famous Bollywood actress and model
Maharaja	Hindu ruler
Maharashtran	India's third largest state
Malayali	a person from Kerala in South India

mandap	the religious structure under which Hindus marry
mangalsutra	traditional gold and onyx wedding necklace that the bride wears when she marries
mangalsutra bandhan	where the bride and groom tie a religious thread around one another during the wedding ceremony
masala	mix of spices for Indian dishes
mendhi	skin decoration
mendhi party	when women gather to have their hands and feet decorated with intricate body paint before the wedding
Mira Nair	famous film director
Mississippi Masala	1991 film directed by Mira Nair starring Denzel Washington
mithai	Indian sweets
Modern Bride	wedding planning magazine targeting middle-to-upper class mainstream American women
Monsoon Wedding	2001 Bollywood movie directed by Mira Nair
mughal	member of a dynasty
mukut	crown on the turban
Mumbai	Bombay
N.R.I.	Non-Resident Indian
naan	popular Indian bread
Nehru suit	popular type of men's formal wear in India
occasional Hindus	term used to describe the second generation that participates in Hindu rituals only on occasion, usually during rites of passage such as getting engaged and married
pakoras	type of Indian appetizer
palak paneer	spinach side dish
pluralistic	religion that pays homage to more than one deity
prasad	sweet substance offered to an idol before consumed
puja	a religious ritual that Hindus perform on a variety of occasions to pray or show respect to God (also spelled as pooja)
pulloh	Hindi word for skirt
Punjab	state in India
puti	type of Indian bread
rakhis	threaded bracelets women tie on their brother and cousin-brother's hands at the religious holiday Rakhi

Ritu Kumar	Indian fashion designer
roti	type of Indian bread
Salman Rushdie	Indian-born fiction writer and essayist
salwaar-kameeze	a matching tunic and pant outfit commonly worn by women for everyday use and informal occasions
samosas	potato, rice and pea-filled dumplings
sangeet	a pre-wedding party where family members entertain one another with song and dance
sanyasa	search for spiritual truth, which may involve actively renouncing society
sapta-padi	where the couple takes seven steps together around the sacred fire at their wedding ceremony
sari	popular formal Indian women's clothing
second generation	U.S.-born children of the immigrant generation
shaadi	Hindi word for marriage
Shaadi Style	Indian bridal magazine
Shaadi.com	Internet matrimonial website
Shruti	New York University's secular cultural group for students of South Asian ethnic heritage
social and cultural criteria	Maira's term for a superficial body of knowledge about secular subjects such as Bollywood films, Indian music, bhangra dance, and foreign language skills
suswgatam	where the bride's mother welcomes and the bride garlands the groom
Swaminarayan	Hindu sect
symbolic ethic American capital	the quality of a person when they act, speak, or dress in an American manner
symbolic ethic Indian capital	the quality of a person when they act, speak, or dress in an Indian manner
symbolic ethnicity	term from Gans's "Symbolic Ethnicity" (1979) which describes how second- and third-generation Europeans living in America participate in ceremonies that celebrate rites of passage using consumer goods, [and] notable foods [that act] as ethnic symbols
tabla	Indian drums
Telugu	group of South Indians who share the same language

tikka	round dot of make-up on a woman's forehead
tumeric	yellow paste popularly used in Indian cooking
Twinkle Khanna	Indian film actress
Uttar Pradesh	northern province in India
vanaprasthya	retirement stage
varmala	the bride and groom place a garland on one another
Vera Wang	high-end bridal gown designer
WeddingSutra.com	wedding planning website for Indian women
yoga	a form of exercise focused on stretching that is believed to have developed in India

Bibliography

Agarwal, Priya. *Passage From India: Post-1965 Indian Immigrants and their Children*. California: Yuvati Publications, 1991.

Ahmed, Kauser. "Adolescent Development for South Asian American Girls." *Emerging Voices: South Asian American Women Redefine Self, Family, and Community*. Ed. Saneeta R. Gupta. London: Alta Mira Press, 1999. 37-49.

Althen, Gary. *American Ways: A Guide for Foreigners in the United States*. New York: Intercultural Press, 1988.

Bacon, Jean. *Life Lines: Community, Family and Assimilation among Asian Indian Immigrants*. New York: Oxford University Press, 1996.

Bailey, Beth. *From Front Porch to Back Seat: Courtship in Twentieth-Century America*. Baltimore: The Johns Hopkins University Press, 1988.

Bhachu, Parminder. *Dangerous Designs: Asian Women Fashion the Diaspora Economies*. New York: Routledge, 2004.

Desai, Jigna. *Beyond Bollywood: The Cultural Politics of South Asian Diasporic Film*. New York: Routledge, 2004.

Egan, Jennifer. "Love in the Time of No Time." *New York Times*, 23 November 2003, 67.

Espiritu, Yen Le. *Asian American Women and Men: Labor, Laws, and Love*. CA: AltaMira Press, 2000.

Flood, Gain. *An Introduction to Hinduism*. Cambridge: Cambridge University Press, 1996.

Gans, Herbert J. "Second-generation decline: scenarios for the economic and ethnic futures of the post-1965 American immigrants." *Ethnic and Racial Studies* Volume 15 Number 2 April 1992. 173-189.

Gans, Herbert J. "Symbolic Ethnicity: Future of Ethnic Groups and Cultures in America." *Ethnic and Racial Studies* 2(1): 1-20. Routledge & Kegan Paul Ltd: January 1979.

Geertz, Clifford. *Interpretation of Culture*. Basic Books, 1973.

Gupta, Sangeeta. "Walking on Edge: Indian-American Women Speak Out on Dating and Marriage." *Emerging Voices: South Asian American Women Redefine Self, Family, and Community*. Ed. Sangeeta R. Gupta. London: Alta Mira Press, 1999. 120-145.

Halter, Marilyn. *Shopping for Identity: The Marketing of Ethnicity*. New York:

Schocken Books, 2000.

Herberg, Will. *Protestant-Catholic-Jew: An Essay in American Religious Sociology*. Chicago: University of Chicago Press, 1983.

Hess, Gary R. "The Forgottten Asian Americans: The East Indian Community in the United States." Ed. Franklin Ng. *The History and Immigration of Asian Americans*. New York: Garland Publishing, Inc., 1998. 106-126.

Joshi, Khyati Y. *New Roots in America's Sacred Ground: Religion, Race, and Ethnicity in Indian America*. New Brunswick, New Jersey: Rutgers University Press, 2006.

Kalita, S. Mitra. *Suburban Sahibs: Three Immigrant Families and their Passage from India to America*. New Jersey: Rutgers University Press, 2005.

Kendall, Laurel. *Getting Married in Korea: Of Gender, Morality, and Modernity*. Berkeley: University of California Press, 1996.

Khandelwal, Madhulika S. *Becoming American, Being Indian: An Immigrant Community in New York City*. Ithaca: Cornell University Press, 2002.

Kibria, Nazli. *Becoming Asian American: Second Generation Chinese and Korean American Identities*. Baltimore: The Johns Hopkins University Press, 2002.

Kibria, Nazli. *Family Tightrope: The Changing Lives of Vietnamese Americans*. Princeton: Princeton University Press, 1993.

Kibria, Nazli, 1996. "Not Asian, Black or White? Reflections on South Asian American Racial Identity." *Amerasia Journal* 22:2: 77-86.

Kibria, Nazli. "South Asian Americans." Ed. Pyong Gap Min. *Asian Americans: Contemporary Trends and Issues*. CA: Sage Publications, 2005. 206-227.

Klostermaier, Klaus K. *A Survey of Hinduism*. Albany: State of University of New York Press, 1994.

Kurien, Prema. "Becoming American by Becoming Hindu: Indian Americans Take Their Place at the Multicultural Table." *Gatherings in Diaspora: Religious Communities and the New Immigration*. Ed. R. Stephen Warner and Judith G. Wittner. Philadelphia: Temple University, 1998.

Lahiri, Jhumpa. *The Namesake*. Great Britain: Harper Perennial, 2004.

Leonard, Karen. "The Management of Desire: Sexuality and Marriage for Young South Asian Women in America." *Emerging Voices: South Asian American Women Redefine Self, Family, and Community*. Ed. Saneeta R. Gupta. London: Alta Mira Press, 1999. 107-119.

Leonard, Karen Isaksen. *The South Asian Americans*. Westport, Connecticut: Greenwood Press, 1997.

Lessinger, Johanna. *From the Ganges to the Hudson: Indian Immigrants in New York City*. Boston: Allyn and Bacon, 1995.

Lipner, Julius. *Hindus: Their religious beliefs and practices*. London: Routledge, 1994.

Maira, Sunaina Marr. *Desis in the House: Indian American Youth Culture in New York City*. Philadelphia: Temple University Press, 2002.

Mauss, Marcel. *The Gift: The form and reason for exchange in Archaic Societies*. New York: W.W. Norton, 1990.

Mazumdar, Shampa and Sanjoy Mazumdar. "Creating the Sacred: Altars in the

Hindu American Home." *Revealing the Sacred*. Eds. Jane Naomi Iwamura and Paul Spickard. New York: Routledge, 2003. 143-158.

Michaels, Axel. *Hinduism: Past and Present*. Princeton: Princeton University Press, 1998.

Min, Pyong Gap. *Asian Americans: Contemporary Trends and Issues*. CA: Sage Publications, 1995.

Mukhi, Sunita. *Doing the Desi Things: Performing Indianness in New York City*. New York: Garland Publishing, Inc., 2000.

Nimbark, Ashakant. "Chapter 6: Hinduism in New York City." Eds. Tony Carnes and Anna Karpathakis. *New York Glory: Religions in the City*. New York: New York University Press, 2001.

Otnes, Cele C. and Elizabeth H. Pleck. *Cinderella Dreams: The Allure of the Lavish Wedding*. Los Angeles: University of California Press, 2003.

Perry, Alex. "Land of the Wedding Planners: Indias elite are used to throwing lavish weddings. But is there a cost to all this fun?" *Time* 27 February 2006, 46.

Prashad, Vijay. *The Karma of Brown Folk*. Minneapolis: University of Minnesota Press, 2000.

Purkayastha, Bandana. *Negotiating Ethnicity: Second-Generation South Asian Americans Traverse a Transnational World*. New Jersey: Rutgers University Press, 2005.

Raj, Dhooleka S. *Where are you from? Middle-Class Migrants in the Modern World*. "Chapter 5: The Search for a Suitable Boy," 105-136. Los Angeles: University of California Press, 2003.

Saran, Parmatma. *The Asian Indian Experience in the United States*. Cambridge: Schenkman Publishing Company, Inc., 1985.

Shukla, Sandhya. *India Abroad: Diasporic Cultures of Postwar America and England*. Princeton: Princeton University Press, 2003.

Stevens, Gillian and Mary E.M. McKillip and Hiromi Ishzawa. "Intermarriage in the Second Generation: Choosing Between Newcomers and Natives," *Special Issue: The Second Generation in the United States*, http://www.-migrationinformation.org/Feature/display.cfm?ID=444 (October 2006).

Swidler, Ann. *Talking of Love: How Culture Matters*. Chicago: The University of Chicago Press, 2001.

U.S. Department of Commerce, *The Asian American Community: 2004* (Washington D.C.: U.S. Census Bureau, February 2007), 8.

U.S. Department of Commerce, *We the People: Asians in the United States*, December 2004. Washington D.C.: U.S. Census Bureau, 2004.

Waters, Mary C. *Ethnic Options: Choosing Identities in America*. Berkeley: University of California Press, 1990.

Williams, Raymond Bradbury, ed. *Sacred Thread: Modern Transmissions of Hindu Traditions in India and Abroad*. PA: ANIMA Publications, 1992.

Williams, Raymond Bradbury. *Religions of Immigrants from India and Pakistan: New Threads in the American Tapestry*. Cambridge: Cambridge University Press, 1988.

Zhou, Min. 1997. "Growing Up American: The Challenge Confronting Immigrant Children and Children of Immigrants." *Annual Review of Sociology* 23: 63-95.

Index

About the Author

Kavita Ramdya was born in New York City and raised in Long Island. She holds a BA from New York University and an MA and PhD from Boston University. Publication credits include *India Abroad*, *The Indian-American*, and the *Colombia Journal of American Studies*. She currently lives with her husband in London.